BREAD CRUMBS

AMY FRIESEN

BREAD CRUMBS

FROM HOME CARE TO CARE HOMES

A FAMILY'S GUIDE *THROUGH* THE ELDERCARE JOURNEY

Copyright © 2024 Amy Friesen

All rights reserved. No part of this publication may be reproduced, distributed, or transmitted in any form or by any means, including photocopying, recording, or other electronic or mechanical methods, without the prior written permission of the publisher, except in the case of brief quotations embodied in critical reviews and certain other noncommercial uses permitted by copyright law. For permission requests, write to the publisher, addressed "Attention: Permissions Coordinator," at the address below.

Eldercare
Publishing
Co.

eldercarepublishingco@gmail.com

ISBN: 978-1-7772351-1-6 (paperback)
ISBN: 978-1-7772351-2-3 (ebook)
ISBN: 978-1-7772351-3-0 (hardcover)
ISBN: 978-1-7772351-4-7 (audiobook)

Ordering Information:
Special discounts are available on quantity purchases by corporations, associations, and others. For details, contact eldercarepublishingco@gmail.com

TABLE OF CONTENTS

From the Author   i
Introduction   xi
Trends and Challenges in the Senior-Living Industry   xi

Part 1: New and Unfamiliar Territory

Chapter 1: *Navigating Generational Dynamics: Advocacy Amid Shifting Roles*   3
Chapter 2: *Life Blueprint Design: Creating a Cohesive Environment of Caring*   9
Chapter 3: *Caring Through Chaos: Nurturing Well-Being amid Guilt and Burnout*   15
Chapter 4: *Building Bridges: Initiating Conversations on Eldercare*   25
Chapter 5: *Eldercare Red Flags*   37

Part 2: Preplanning

Chapter 6: *Laying the Foundation: Carepath Planning*   47
Chapter 7: *Understanding the Retirement Living Industry*   69
Chapter 8: *Understanding the Long-Term Care Industry*   81
Chapter 9: *Remaining in the Community Safely: Strategies for Success*   93
Chapter 10: *Opening the Lines of Communication*   113
Chapter 11: *Seniors with Dementia: Strategies for Success*   137

Final Words   157
Where Are They Now?   159
About the Author   163
Appendix   165

Dedication

To all the caregivers who feel unseen. I see you. Your tireless dedication and unwavering love are important and valued. This book is for you. You are making a profound difference in the lives you touch, and your efforts are deeply appreciated. Remember, you are doing the best you can, and that is enough.

FROM THE AUTHOR

Hey, I'm Amy.

This is a note to tell you I see you. Yes, you. The struggles in Eldercare are real and are definitely not given the attention they deserve. Both caregivers and seniors grow into a position where they need to navigate completely foreign territory. If they aren't successful, the results could be deadly.

Before the 1950s (-ish), elders were housed in institutions that were designed for criminals. These became overcrowded with people who could not care for themselves, including the poor and mentally ill.[1]

If you think about it, the senior-housing system we currently have in Canada for long-term care has only existed in its current form since approximately the 1950s, and retirement homes came after that. These dates would insinuate that the average family has had little to no involvement in this type of care for their elders. I believe it will take multiple

---

[1] Barbara Emodi, "A History of Long-Term Facilities for the Elderly in Canada" (working paper, CMHC Nursing Home and Hostels Design Guidelines Study, A. W. Cluff and P. J. Cluff Architects and Planners, July 1977), https://publications.gc.ca/collections/collection_2016/schl-cmhc/NH18-25-4-1977-eng.pdf.

generations for this type of housing to become commonplace and completely comprehended. In the same span of time, people have *just* begun to live longer due to medical advances, better housing, food, and other factors. In 1950, the general life expectancy was 69 years old, and the public was crying out for better standards for nursing homes. Today, the general life expectancy is 81 years old, and the housing system is still not keeping up.[2]

We are now at the beginning of the baby boom era in senior living, and we are already feeling the extreme pinch as these folks begin to need and search out care. Combining this with the COVID years, there is a huge influx of people not just needing but *requiring* congregate-living settings such as long-term care and retirement living. But alas, the long-term care homes are full and have waiting lists, and as I write this, the retirement homes have very low or no availability on care floors either. The system is in trouble, and it always has been. Although standards in housing have gotten better over time, the amount of housing with care available has been drastically underestimated.

So, Amy, why are you telling me this? Great question! All this is to say that people are really hard on themselves when it comes to caring for those they love. This stage in life can be very stressful, and when you combine that with foreign emotions

---

[2] "Life Expectancy, 1920–1922 to 2009–2011," Statistics Canada, last updated May 17, 2018, https://www150.statcan.gc.ca/n1/pub/11-630-x/11-630-x2016002-eng.htm.

FROM THE AUTHOR

such as guilt and grief, time crunches, lack of availability, family dynamics, and money, people are really struggling.

Let me tell you a little more about myself to give you some context as to why I am so passionate about helping seniors, caregivers, and the senior-housing industry.

But first, a story.

A few years back, I went through the ordeal of trying to find day care for my daughter and riding the emotional roller coaster that process caused.

If you have ever gone through this, or even had the similar experience of leaving your child with a sitter, then you will understand the emotions associated. If not, let me tell you more.

At this point in my life, my day-to-day job was being a business owner. I worked full-time and considered myself an expert in my field. I was a bright, resourceful individual and expected that this step of securing day care would be like any other decision. Step 1: Find available day care. Step 2: Enroll Eva. Step 3: Go about my life. I'm pretty sure I can hear you laughing already.

What I didn't count on was the shortage of day care, the waiting lists, the emotions that accompanied leaving my daughter with strangers, and the ongoing need to remain available while she was there in case of issues or emergencies.

BREADCRUMBS

Although senior living is not like day care, in a sense, it is. Let me rephrase that: the emotions are the same.

The day I had to make a decision about which day care to bring my 10-month-old daughter to was the day that I more fully understood how adult children of seniors see the senior-living mountain in front of them. And it does seem like a mountain: huge and looming, with twists and turns and lots of unknowns.

How will they take care of my loved one? Is there enough care for my loved one? What will my loved one be doing during the day? Will my loved one make friends? Will they be sociable or isolated? What will the food be like, and will they like it? Can I fit this into my monthly budget? And, perhaps most profoundly, *Will I be able to step back without feeling guilty and let the staff at this new place take care of my loved one?*

If you have raised children, then you are in luck. Many of you have transferable skills that you honed years ago to assist your senior loved ones. Drawing on your life skills from other experiences is going to make you more equipped to handle the challenges of Eldercare. These are some of the transferable skills:

Patience. Both roles demand immense patience. Raising children involves understanding their developmental stages, while caregiving for an aging loved

FROM THE AUTHOR

one may require patience in dealing with health-related issues and changes in behavior or mood.

Time management and organization. Balancing multiple responsibilities, schedules, and priorities is inherent in both roles. Raising kids involves managing school, extracurricular activities, and household tasks. Similarly, caregiving may involve medical appointments, medication schedules, and household management.

Communication. Effective communication is vital in both scenarios. As a parent, you learn to adapt your communication style to your child's age and understanding. Similarly, when caregiving for a loved one, clear and empathetic communication is crucial.

Problem-solving. The ability to troubleshoot and find solutions is honed while raising children. This skill translates well into the role of a caregiver, where you might encounter various challenges related to health care, daily living, or emotional support for your aging loved one.

Adaptability. Being flexible and adaptable in different situations is key. As a parent, you learn to adjust your approach as your child grows. Similarly, caregiving often demands adapting to the changing health conditions and evolving needs of an elderly loved one.

In addition to transferable skills, you will also have experiences that will feel similar, thus equipping you to remember how you dealt with not only the situations but also the feelings in the past.

Transferable experiences include the day care example I mentioned earlier, assisting with activities of daily living (including dressing, bathing, assisting with transfers, and perineal care), and handling the health-care system. In both roles, you will also learn advocacy and decision-making. These skills are invaluable when advocating for your loved one's care and making crucial health-care or financial decisions.

As a professional in the senior-living industry for the last 20 years, I have helped families work through their questions and struggles. I have learned how to support people in getting their emotions to a place where they can minimize the stress and guilt associated with helping their loved ones find senior-living options that fit their needs. I've helped thousands of seniors come to a place of peace where they can manage expectations and truly understand their options.

Early in my career as a marketer in local retirement homes, I had the pleasure of working with seniors directly as they explored retirement living. Sadly, although the homes were nice and I was perfectly pleasant, those seniors often went home feeling frustrated, sad, and overwhelmed. Many times, the seniors chose to do nothing

FROM THE AUTHOR

at all instead of doing what the industry was requiring of them, which was to take on more information that (a) they didn't want and (b) they didn't understand. Often, when I would follow up with those seniors, I would learn that they had ended up in the hospital, in long-term care, or most sadly, passed away.

My experience in the industry made me painfully aware of the huge gap that exists in the system. Let's face it: seniors are falling through the cracks, and the system is not supporting them or their families.

I had all these seniors and their families in mind when I developed my company, Tea & Toast. I knew there had to be a better way to help families get the information they needed without being bombarded by unwanted emails and phone calls.

I've learned a lot on my Tea & Toast journey. The most critical piece of advice I can share is this: It all boils down to strategy. What is your strategy? Beyond what the situation is today, have you thought—honestly—about what things might look like for you and your loved one, say, three years from now? Two years from now? Or even next year?

Making a plan in the early days and revisiting it as things change are really what set families up for success. If everyone were open to discussing their wishes in advance, and if people chose to *strategize* rather than having to react to something unexpected, I truly believe that we would have far fewer crisis situations. Another bonus to strategizing is that, in a crisis situation (for example, a bad fall that sends a senior to the hospital), the senior's loved ones would know exactly what to do and where to turn because a solid plan would already be in place.

Strategizing gives families clarity about potential needs, knowledge of the financial plan, ability to balance responsibilities among other family members, and dignity for their loved one. When you can respect preferences and choices regarding care, many emotions settle down and don't carry as much weight. I can't tell you how often I hear "My mom won't tell me her preferences and just wants me to take care of things." Scenarios of this nature induce significant stress and unease for caregivers and are often overlooked or inadequately addressed. Creating a plan offers long-term sustainability that you can adjust as needs and circumstances change.

So, what will you get from this book? On a practical level, it will provide you with a lot of information, address concerns you may have, and offer some strategies and action plans. On an emotional level, my hope for this book is that it will help you to understand that you are not alone and that many, many people face similar situations.

FROM THE AUTHOR

My final piece of advice is to take care of yourself. Caregiver burnout is real. Take note of the situation you and your loved one are in, and make sure to implement safeguards to ensure you are able to also care for yourself. There are certain things that you can't get back once they're gone, and your health is at the top of the list. Be good to yourself.

I hope you find this book helpful and that you gain at least a little relief knowing that you are not the only one in the world dealing with these issues, even though it may sometimes feel that way.

XOX,
Amy

INTRODUCTION

Trends and Challenges in the Senior-Living Industry

With an ever-growing and never-ending to-do list, it's no wonder that the average adult feels overwhelmed and stressed these days.

Between their own personal responsibilities of work, self-care (who are we kidding, what self-care?) and family obligations like groceries, meals, homework, soccer practice, music lessons, and family time, the average person is maxed out. There simply aren't enough hours in a day.

To add fuel to the fire, as baby boomers age and begin to require more care, their adult children tend to take on many different roles, such as personal caregiver, housekeeper, meal preparer, delivery person, and chauffeur. An increasing number of individuals are also finding themselves in the sandwich generation, stuck between caring for their aging parents *and* their own children.

BREADCRUMBS

Although tasks such as bringing Mom and Dad some leftovers a few times a week and driving to appointments here and there can seem manageable at first, this balance isn't sustainable for the long term. As the senior's needs increase and their capabilities decrease, loved ones are often left holding the bag, becoming the main—and sometimes only—source of care for their parents.

And what about those caregivers who are caring from a distance? There are an awful lot of families who are spread out, not only across North America but the entire world as well. Many of these family members do want to be involved in these conversations, but distance makes it difficult. Being at a distance makes it hard for caregivers or family members to stay informed about the situation, including the level of care needed or the overall conditions. At times, families are also dealing with the opposite: those at a distance who feel that they know more than the caregiving sibling living nearby. This often causes a lot of issues when decisions need to be made. I have personally seen this situation several times, and it tends to play out the exact same way. The local sibling advocates for long-term care, while the distant sibling believes their family member is capable of remaining in the home. But the local sibling is often trumped by the distant sibling because what many seniors—and people in general—would prefer is to stay in their own homes. If any family member agrees that they're

INTRODUCTION

still independent, this is what many seniors hold on to, as opposed to making a plan and understanding that they may actually be at risk currently.

Because of this, more and more caregivers are becoming burned out, forcing themselves through the day in order to care for loved ones and avoid the feelings of guilt, grief, and exhaustion that they may have.

> Caregiver burnout is a state of physical, emotional, and mental exhaustion that may be accompanied by a change in attitude—from positive and caring to negative and unconcerned. Burnout can occur when caregivers do not get the help they need, or if they try to do more than they are able—either physically or financially. Caregivers who are "burned out" may experience fatigue, stress, anxiety, and depression. Many caregivers also feel guilty if they spend time on themselves rather than on their ill or elderly loved one.[3]

Let's be sure of this: Most of my clients—close to 90%—are either experiencing some form of burnout or are just about to. Part of the problem is that burnout isn't recognized for what it is. Many people think, *I can manage this—it's only temporary*. However, what often happens is that the amount

---

3   "Recognizing Caregiver Burnout," WebMD, last updated January 11, 2022, https://www.webmd.com/healthy-aging/caregiver-recognizing-burnout.

of care being provided to a loved one increases, and the situation lasts longer than originally anticipated. Before a caregiver is even aware of what is happening, they find themselves deeper than they may have originally planned and struggling to hold on to their own sense of identity and purpose, not to mention their health.

To stay on top of this, it is important to make time to care for yourself as well. However, it's not always that easy, as there is often a lot of caregiver guilt associated with caring for yourself when others in your life also require care. It can feel as if everyone wants a piece of you and as if you should put their needs ahead of yours.

From my own point of view, I can tell you that guarding personal time is often difficult. My life is a balancing act: caring for a young family and several household pets, worrying about my parents who are not living in the same city as me, and running a growing business with employees. In my business life, I often find myself taking on what can be intense emotions from my clients. I'm constantly in problem-solving mode. If you work in a caring profession, you're most likely very aware of this experience of compassion fatigue, although many wouldn't recognize the definition.

According to WebMD, "compassion fatigue is a term that describes the physical, emotional, and psychological

INTRODUCTION

impact of helping others."[4] Finding the extra time for just oneself *and* taking it without all the stress and guilt weighing on us is difficult.

I encourage you to be mindful and watch for the signs, not only for yourself but also for any parent or loved one who may be in a caregiving role. There are many resources available in your community to help those dealing with compassion fatigue. However, to find them, you have to first recognize and accept what is happening. I have included some helpful resources at the end of this book.

Many adult children and seniors find Eldercare planning and making a strategy for the future completely overwhelming. For instance, many seniors don't want to have these important conversations with their loved ones because they're scared of the changes that may need to occur or they have other objections that have not quite been identified (more on this in chapter 4). And for the adult children, many don't want to have to broach the awkward conversations that Eldercare often brings with it, such as living situations, finance, and end-of-life planning. At the end of the day, many families find it easier to keep their heads in the sand, and often, because of that lack of planning, many seniors and their families find themselves in

---

4   "Compassion Fatigue: Symptoms to Look For," WebMD, last updated December 12, 2022, https://www.webmd.com/mental-health/signs-compassion-fatigue.

crisis, not actually having access to as many choices as they would have had they planned in the first place. When a senior ends up in crisis, it often means all hands on deck, and the research and planning that would have been spread out over months—if not years—end up compacted into as little time as one week. Additionally, when a crisis happens for a senior, a crisis also happens for their caregivers. As you may expect, crisis management is very time consuming and stressful. If being proactive could save you and your loved ones an immense amount of time and emotional upset, wouldn't you want to plan?

I have been fortunate to work with thousands of families and assist them through their Eldercare journeys, whether they were looking to remain at home and wanted to know how to stay safe, or they wanted to know how to choose the best retirement home or understand long-term care. Whatever their goals, many families find the whole process physically and emotionally draining.

Before you can decide on a set of strategies to assist your loved one throughout the Eldercare journey, you must first acknowledge the situation your family is in and what you are looking for. Starting here will help you develop the specific strategies you will need to put in place.

In the following chapters, you will learn about the terminology that will begin to take over your life as your loved

INTRODUCTION

one ages, whether it is in the community when bringing in extra services, through a trip to the hospital, or when exploring senior-living. Additionally, my hope is that I can teach you strategies and ways to think about different situations, which will arm you with as much education and information as possible in the hopes that you will feel more confident and at ease in your decision-making process throughout the Eldercare journey.

Buckle up, and let's take on this journey together!

PART 1:
NEW AND UNFAMILIAR TERRITORY

CHAPTER 1:

NAVIGATING GENERATIONAL DYNAMICS

Advocacy Amid Shifting Roles

You're not the child, friend, or partner anymore. You have now morphed into a new position that comes with immense responsibilities and requires time and emotional bandwidth. Most often, caregiving is not something people have planned on doing. However, most of us will find ourselves there at one time or another. Nowadays, the average family is becoming more likely to be caring for people on both ends of the spectrum, with children who are still reliant on caregivers as well as aging parents who now need additional support. This generation of families has been termed the sandwich generation. I have even had an individual call herself a "club sandwich," caring for her child, her mom, and her spouse who had an illness.

In Canada, there are over seven million seniors, and this population will continue to grow for the next 20 years.

BREADCRUMBS

This demographic has now outgrown the population aged under 15, and this will dictate how we move forward as a society.[5] To pair with this, the number of caregivers will also have to increase for two main reasons: (1) their loved ones are living longer than ever before, and (2) there simply isn't enough care in the system to help. Based on an analysis of Statistics Canada data there are over 5.2 million caregivers who are also employed full-time.[6] Gone are the days when a stay-at-home adult cared for children and elderly relatives. With the current economy, most families require a dual income, which means caregiving hours are on top of—and most often mixed into—the 40-plus-hour weekly work schedule. One other reality is also at play. Many work environments offer employee assistance programs. However, the focus of these plans tends to be on children, not for caring for elderly family members. Our society has designed care relief around young children, and with the immense number of adult children needing to take time off—including sick days and extended absences from work—to care for their loved ones, our society is in quite a pickle.

---

5 "Older Adults And Population Aging Statistics," Statistics Canada, last updated April 25, 2024, https://www.statcan.gc.ca/en/subjects-start/older_adults_and_population_aging.

6 Andrew Magnaye et al., "Employed Caregivers in Canada: Infographic Series Based on Analyses of Statistics Canada's 2018 General Social Survey on Caregiving and Care Receiving," Research on Aging, Policies, and Practice, University of Alberta, May 2023, https://rapp.ualberta.ca/wp-content/uploads/sites/49/2023/05/Employed-Caregivers-in-Canada-Infographic-Series-Compilation_2023-05-15.pdf.

NAVIGATING GENERATIONAL DYNAMICS

As with any new role, Eldercare comes with a learning curve. In Eldercare, this learning curve is substantial, and as mentioned earlier, if one does not master the information, it could have dire consequences. There are so many things that can go wrong health-wise with any of us, and adding that to increasing housing issues and the general unknowns of aging, many families are not equipped to handle the next stage that is now on their doorsteps.

Currently throughout the world, health-care systems are complicated, and in the Canadian health-care system, it is imperative not only to understand what is happening with yourself or your loved one but also to advocate constantly, as many health-care providers do not take a holistic look at the entire situation, may not fully understand all of the moving pieces, or are just too busy to give the situation the attention it deserves. Many of us have had to advocate for ourselves in the past—however, advocating for an aging loved one adds a layer of unknown and stress that many won't be prepared for. Often, advocating looks like repeating yourself over and over to anyone and everyone who will listen, spinning your wheels, and becoming exhausted with the repetitive action. The truly sad reality is that, regardless of how exhausting advocating can be, it must be done. Without it, your loved one will not receive the care they need, be it in their home, in a hospital, or in a senior-living institution. You literally have to stay on top of things 24/7.

To top this off, one of the truly frustrating parts of obtaining information are the silos in the health-care system. The public system (hospitals, long-term care, and governmental agencies) does not do a good job of understanding the private sector (home care and retirement homes) and thus tends to stick to recommendations in only the public sector, which greatly limits the options available for families. I can't tell you how often I have tried to work with government agencies to deliver education in conjunction with them, only to be told that, because I run a private company, they are not allowed to collaborate with me. What the government doesn't seem to understand is that, without the private care and housing system, they would be in a lot more trouble. There is a much better way to assist families. However, it will take the government listening, learning, and working together, not only with the private sector but also with families.

The other aspect of navigating generational dynamics is adjusting to evolving family structures and understanding intergenerational differences.

Communication and empathy play important parts in shifting roles, establishing new routines, and understanding decision-making. Traditionally, many families lived intergenerationally, with several generations caring for each other under one roof. These living arrangements are dwindling.

NAVIGATING GENERATIONAL DYNAMICS

Today, it's often more common to see arrangements where the nuclear family cares for each other and the extended family of grandparents and great-grandparents live in separate houses and even in separate areas, making family caregiving all that much more difficult.

As for decision-making, the seniors of today grew up in less forward-thinking, open families where many things went undiscussed, such as care needs, money, and future planning. Often, these items were seen as taboo, making it challenging when the older generation was faced with caring for their aging loved ones. Today, it is still challenging for the now-adult children to try to navigate the same care and housing dilemmas for their senior loved ones. It will be important to remember when navigating the Eldercare journey that things may not always be smooth sailing and that decisions may be made that don't make sense to you as a caregiver. It will be more important than ever before to keep the lines of communication open to navigate the ups and downs. More on communication in chapter 10.

As you can see, there are many moving parts when roles shift, and the emotions and responsibilities that come with these shifting roles can be overwhelming. Remember, you are not alone, and many, many people are also participating in this shift.

KEY TAKEAWAYS

1. As more seniors come of age, it's never been more important to plan out how you can incorporate your loved one's needs into your nuclear family. The current health-care system simply does not accommodate in the ways that families require.

2. The Eldercare journey requires a substantial amount of advocating to establish a plan that looks at an individual's needs holistically.

CHAPTER 2:

LIFE BLUEPRINT DESIGN

Creating a Cohesive Environment of Caring

When the day comes that your loved one requires care, it can sometimes mean all hands-on deck. Many caregivers jump in with both feet, only to find themselves still with two feet in months—even years—later. The problem is that no one really knows how long caregiving will last, how much stress it will cause, and how long the caregiver will have to put their own life on hold. Because things are never written in stone, it is difficult to establish a solid new routine that includes caregiving. If the upcoming caregiving was planned, then a new set of routines, habits, and boundaries would have been established to keep all the moving pieces in orbit. When caregiving has not been planned, it can be tricky to establish these three things—however, that doesn't mean that it's still not important to do so.

Breaking it down, let's look at ways to be a caregiver without losing yourself in caring. After all, we all only have one life to live, and we all deserve to be as happy and functional as possible. I call this strategy the Life Blueprint. It looks at ways to set boundaries, improve routines, and create habits while caring for your loved one, all without losing yourself in caregiving.

SETTING BOUNDARIES

Boundaries are one of those things that are essential in life. Setting boundaries protects you and teaches people how to treat you. You can set boundaries for almost anything—you can set emotional boundaries, physical boundaries, time boundaries, etc. While caregiving, there are many situations that can arise that the loved one you are caring for may need assistance with. However, it is important to know what you have the mental and physical capacity to take on and what you do not.

Boundaries that are useful to set include time expectations and physical care expectations. There are a variety of reasons to set these boundaries. Below, I will cover some situations for which a boundary would be helpful to protect yourself from overcommitting and burning out.

Time Expectations

Time expectations can get out of control very quickly. Sometimes, the loved one you are caring for doesn't realize they are asking for more time than you are able to give, especially when a boundary hasn't been set. The best way to set this type of boundary is to openly communicate and assert your personal preferences and protect against having them compromised or violated. It is essential to prioritize what you need and to protect the time required. Where do you feel strapped for time? What are your priorities, and how do you put yourself first? I know this may sound foreign to you, as many caregivers feel selfish for prioritizing themselves while being caregivers. But let me ask if you don't prioritize and care for yourself, who will?

My favorite way to explain this is by using the instructions we receive on airplanes as an analogy. Put your own oxygen mask on before assisting others.

It is equally important to also schedule personal time in your calendar. This allows you to fit yourself into your day and to ensure that what you need to get done actually gets done. Prioritize yourself and book them into your schedule.

Habits and Routines

Both habits and routines are regular and repeated actions. Habits happen without conscious thought, and routines often require more intention and effort to build. Both are valuable for caregivers.

BREADCRUMBS

When you first take on the role of caregiver, it is natural to let habits and routines slip or even sometimes vanish. However, your habits and routines are a part of what makes you, well, you. Often, our routines are doing things to care for ourselves, such as working out and getting enough sleep. It is no surprise that when caregiving starts to become more involved, our sleep patterns can get jumbled—and that's not even getting into the sleepless nights, tossing and turning, and worrying. It's really important to hang on to your routines or, if you don't have routines yet, to *form* routines to help you through the caregiving process. After all, caregivers are often caregiving for a number of years. Is not taking care of yourself for years a good option for you?

Here are a few more reasons why routines are important for caregivers:

- **Reduced stress.** Caregiving can be physically and emotionally demanding. Routines can help reduce stress by providing structure and organization in the caregiver's day. When caregivers have a clear plan in place, they may feel more in control of their responsibilities, which can help alleviate stress and prevent burnout.
- **Time efficiency.** Establishing routines helps caregivers manage their time more efficiently. Knowing

what needs to be done and when it needs to be done can help caregivers prioritize tasks and allocate their time and energy effectively.
- **Improved communication.** Routines can facilitate better communication between the caregiver, the person receiving care, and other members of the caregiving team. When everyone knows what to expect and when to expect it, communication can help prevent misunderstandings and ensure that everyone is on the same page.

Whether you are new to caregiving or have been doing it for years, it's never too late to organize things in your life to serve you and your family better, and that means prioritizing self-care.

KEY TAKEAWAYS

1. Once you become a caregiver, it becomes more important than ever to care for yourself and prioritize your own well-being.

2. Setting up routines and habits is essential for a successful caring relationship.

CHAPTER 3:

CARING THROUGH CHAOS

Nurturing Well-Being amid Guilt and Burnout

I know you know. I also know you know better. As a caregiver myself, I recognize that it isn't easy to "put your oxygen mask on before assisting others." Let's face it: Many of the people we are assisting are our loved ones, parents, children, and partners. These are all the people whom we would do almost anything for, and for many of us, this includes sacrificing our own well-being to maintain theirs. So how do you care for your loved ones without ending up in a health crisis yourself? And how do you put limits on your output and your time without feeling guilty?

"Guilt," that five-letter word that eats at most of us. It often comes when we feel responsible for doing or not doing something. When it comes to our loved ones, this can be overwhelmingly triggering, especially since sometimes, those actions and decisions can mean a big change for our loved ones. Here's an example:

ADULT CHILD

Dad passed away, and Mom is continuing to live in her own home. Dad used to be Mom's caregiver, and with him no longer there to support her, things must change, or Mom will end up in a crisis and most likely in the hospital. As her child, either you can step further into the caregiving role to help Mom sustain her life at home, while putting your own life on hold and possibly not being able to spend as much time with your own family, or you can help her look for a different solution that doesn't involve so much assistance from you.

Becoming her full-time caregiver puts the pressure on you. The guilt will come from things missed at home with your nuclear family or from things you did or didn't do while caregiving for Mom, such as being late or mixing up medication. If you help to bring in home care or look for a retirement home, the guilt trigger will often come from Mom herself, as she may not want to move. Additionally, family and friends' comments are another way that the guilt button can be pressed.

SENIOR PARTNER

A nurse by trade, you are now caring for your husband. His care needs have been increasing slowly over time, but you feel capable of handling his care on your own. But one day, you realize that the care you have been providing for the last five years has taken a toll on your health. You know that you need to take care of yourself—after all, you are a healthcare professional—but you can't let go of being his full-time caregiver. What will people say if you bring in help or move? *I should be able to do this; others do this without my training, and they have a much harder time. My husband doesn't want strangers giving him physical care.* The guilt here comes from the "supposed tos" and the "what-ifs."

The moral of the story is that guilt will find a way to come through, regardless of the path you take. The only way to manage the guilt is to be thoughtful and firm in your decisions and to know that the guilt will need to be managed. Don't live in a situation just because you are "supposed to" be able to do something or because you're wondering "what if" your children have a different opinion.

Now, keeping this in mind, how do you thoughtfully look at a caregiving situation and make the right decision? It all starts with looking at yourself as an individual. What are your preferences, skill sets, mental health needs, and family needs? Next, how do you set yourself up for success where you can come to a place of peace and are not second-guessing your actions? Below are some questions to answer that will start putting the pieces in place. As with anything, it's always best to do this ahead of time so that when the time comes, you know how to react. As you can imagine, many people would not consider these questions, as most often either people are thrust into a caregiving situation, or it sneaks up on them slowly without much notice.

SELF-REFLECTION QUESTIONS

1. How do I see my life unfolding?
2. Do I *want* to be the main caregiver to my loved one?
3. Am I *equipped* to be the main caregiver to my loved one?
4. If I were the main caregiver to my loved one, how would that change my life?
5. Are there things I might miss out on that I would regret if I became a caregiver?

Using the answers you find when asking yourself the questions above, determine the level of caregiving (if any) and the tasks that you are willing to do. If you find that you do not want to be the caregiver (also perfectly acceptable), determine if there are any other tasks you would consider handling for your loved one, such as finances, and consider other ways your loved one could get the care they require (perhaps home care or making a move to a different home) or whether someone else can step up.

If you have made the decision to become a caregiver, when opportunity presents itself there are a few more items that should be considered. Taking note of your answers to the following questions will help set up your new caregiving responsibilities.

WHAT ARE MY BOUNDARIES?

- How much time am I willing to allot to these responsibilities?
- Are there any times of the day that are off limits?
- Are there any care requirements that are off limits? (e.g., bathing)
- Are there any commitments with my family that take priority over my caregiving responsibilities?

These questions will also help you steer clear-ish of caregiver burnout. I'm a believer that there are levels of burnout that individuals experience at different times in their lives. A lot of caregiver burnout boils down to not getting enough time to yourself coupled with being pulled in multiple directions and feeling that you have no control of the situation, layered with new responsibilities and schedules.

When I coach women who are caregivers, there are two strategies that I like to share with them: (1) scheduling personal time and (2) batching. I'll explain more about both.

SCHEDULING PERSONAL TIME

This sounds easy enough, right? That's the trouble. The scheduling is simple—the doing is difficult.

When is the last time that you regularly scheduled something personal in your calendar, besides a doctor's appointment? What about scheduling a recurring massage, a relaxing day at home with no one around, a getaway, or even an hour not to have to get something for someone?

Being a caregiver, you *must* take time to recharge your batteries, and the first step is to carve out time for yourself.

Practice Exercise

Take a minute—don't worry, I'll wait—and choose two things that will make you feel more relaxed or give you energy. Write them into your schedule regularly for the next three months. Additionally, make sure to tell anyone who needs to help block the time for you (e.g., your partner taking the kids out or your adult child coming over to hang out with Grandpa for a bit).

Items could look like these:

- A massage
- A chiropractic session
- An hour to read
- An extra hour of sleep in the morning
- An early bedtime
- A bath
- An hour alone

BATCHING

Another strategy I like using with caregivers is batching. Batching is putting like-items together so that you are not wasting time. Items include tasks, errands, and responsibilities. A great example of this is grocery shopping. Many caregivers are shopping for both their own families' groceries and their parents' but not scheduling them together, which often results in them getting groceries multiple times a week. When batching this task, you only have one list for both households, and can make a plan to tackle the grocery store, saving you very valuable time. Here is an example.

Purchasing groceries for yourself involves these tasks:

1. Checking out the deals
2. Going through cupboards and the fridge
3. Making a list

4. Driving to the store
5. Shopping
6. Forgetting your bags and buying more
7. Driving home
8. Putting away the groceries

If you also need to do the grocery shopping for your parents, most people would double this, not combine it, meaning two trips instead of one, two lists, navigating two stores, etc. It all adds up to wasted time that could be used doing something else…like caring for yourself.

Practice Exercise

Pull out your calendar and schedule time for yourself to go grocery shopping the same day every week. Personally, I like to do this on Thursdays, when the flyers are crisp and fresh! (I digress…) Communicate with your loved one to ask them to make a list of what they need, or on one of your trips to see them, get in the habit of making the list together. Combine this with your shopping list and break it down to types of aisles—for instance, fruit/veg, bakery, meat, dried goods, dairy. Breaking the list down, will save the inevitable back-and-forth that happens when you add a tomato to the bottom of your list and don't see it when you are in the veggie aisle. Make sure to schedule your shopping for a day/time when you will be visiting your loved one afterward avoiding a second trip.

An additional way to tackle shopping specifically is to order online together and pick the groceries up. For a small fee, usually under $5, you can have groceries delivered right to your car, saving even more time. I do this personally as I can add to my online order as I remember things and more thoroughly plan out my meals. Better yet, I can send my husband to pick up the order without $50 more being added by his random grocery store impulses.

Become a detective in your own life and find those time-savers.

I know it seems like a lot of effort to put yourself first and take time to do these techniques, but they work. The goal here is to keep as much of your own energy while giving the rest to those you care for.

KEY TAKEAWAYS

1. Guilt is inevitable. Learn how to dance with it.

2. Taking time to incorporate caregiving into your life will help reduce burnout.

CHAPTER 4:

BUILDING BRIDGES

Initiating Conversations on Eldercare

Regardless of which talk it is, no one really wants to have "the talk." It's awkward and stressful…and did I say *awkward*?

Whether you are teaching your kids about the birds and the bees or discussing end-of-life care decisions with your parents, it's not easy. Conversations regarding Eldercare often carry an added layer of complexity, as it's typically the adult child who needs to initiate these discussions with their parent. This dynamic blurs the boundaries, requiring a delicate balance between assuming a caregiving role and still being the child.

Now, before jumping right in to saying, "Mom, you need to move to a home," or "Dad, it's time to stop spending so much money," and catching your parent off guard, you first need to do some homework. If you want the most successful outcome for both yourself and your loved one, it is imperative to analyze the entire situation.

BREADCRUMBS

Caregiving can often be thrust upon us. There are definitely signs of things to come, but whether people pay attention to those signs depends on how the situation is affecting them personally. Are there situations currently coming up that require more of your attention and effort? Let me give you an example.

ANNA AND MARY

Anna and Mary were two sisters, living their own lives. One lived in Toronto, and the other lived in Ottawa, close to their parents. The topic had been broached with their parents as to how safe they were remaining in their own home. Things weren't going terrifically well for the parents, and the drop-ins from the local daughter had now become almost mandatory so that she could keep an eye on things. The only "talk" they were having at the time was the living arrangements talk, which was not well supported by any other conversations. You see, the living arrangements talk, although great to have, must be intertwined with other conversations that help support the why of what the move is for. Is it a move based on medical reasons, safety, or caregiving responsibilities?

Anna and Mary had gotten their parents to a place where they were considering making a move "but not for a year or more." When I was called to assess and help, here is what I saw:

- Mom had some mild memory loss and was repeating herself. She was the main caregiver for herself and her husband.
- Dad had Parkinson's (although he hadn't had any large shifts in physical issues associated with it yet) and a diagnosis of Lewy body dementia, plus he had recently been in the hospital for atrial fibrillation, hallucinations, and dizziness.
- They had a large home in the country with three flights of stairs and a large lot to care for.
- The family consisted of two daughters: one out of town, the other close enough to be able to check on parents almost daily.

In my opinion, which I shared with the family, it was best that this couple did not remain in their home for another year or more. There were numerous challenges they and their children had not fully considered.

Their father was experiencing two physically debilitating diseases simultaneously, which were both about to worsen, and their mother was taking on the caregiving duties, which included giving him medications at specific time intervals, while struggling with memory impairment herself. Time was of the essence.

Both the daughters knew intellectually that their parents should be looking at a move. However, neither one of them was willing to get into the tough conversations. After all, they had made the step to hire us to assist with the housing search. From a professional point of view, there was still zero urgency to move forward, as they often delayed the search for retirement homes by not responding to emails and phone communication. On top of this, both daughters were stuck in the habit of letting their parents completely drive the ship although both had memory issues. The sisters were having a lot of difficulty with their parents' move from their childhood home and were hell-bent on finding something as similar to their parents' current situation as possible when they did eventually move. This was so much the case that they were adamant about only selecting lower-care homes in a country setting, even though an additional move would be needed imminently, contrary to the professional advice I was offering.

Anna and Mary should have been looking at the entire picture and taking their own personal objections about selling the family home, among other things, off the table because, honestly, they were just clouding the process. Anna and Mary knew they needed help, and they had hired a professional, but they took no professional direction.

In this situation, almost all the talks should have been already started and on the table for discussion. I don't advise that you should have all of the conversations at the same time, however, once others have been started or moved through, you should be able to reference them in this large care puzzle you are trying to put together. Referencing them would have rounded out the entire situation and given depth to the reasons why a move would be a good option.

THE TALKS

Here is a general layout of the seven talks of Eldercare and examples of when each might be used.

The Financial Talk serves multiple purposes, primarily focusing on budgeting, adapting to changes in living situations, and facilitating access to funds. It becomes a pivotal discussion encompassing strategies to manage finances effectively and ensure stability amid shifting circumstances. From allocating resources strategically to navigating changes in lifestyle or housing, this conversation empowers individuals to make informed decisions and optimally harness available financial resources.

The Expectations Talk delves into the mutual understanding and agreement between individuals involved in caregiving roles, addressing the investment of time, financial resources, and responsibilities inherent in providing care. This conversation revolves around crucial aspects such as caregiver time, financial considerations, and the dynamics of caregiving. It serves as a cornerstone for setting realistic expectations, establishing boundaries, and fostering a supportive environment for all parties involved in the caregiving journey.

The Mental Health Talk navigates the complexities of mental well-being, aiming to create a supportive environment where individuals can openly address concerns related to cognitive health, emotional struggles, social isolation, and the intricacies of medication regimens. This conversation tackles a spectrum of critical facets, encompassing discussions on dementia diagnosis, depression, anxiety, isolation, and medication management.

The Physical Health Talk serves as a road map for effectively managing and coordinating physical health support, addressing questions surrounding caregiving responsibilities, scheduling, and the diverse array of tasks essential for maintaining optimal physical well-being. It is a comprehensive discussion centered on aspects including identifying the individuals involved in providing physical care, determining the timing and frequency of their assistance, and outlining specific care needs. By establishing clear communication and understanding regarding the who, when, how often, and what of caregiving, this dialogue ensures a structured and supportive approach to address and fulfill the physical care requirements.

The Living Arrangements Talk aims to prioritize key factors that are crucial in determining living arrangements. By addressing these multifaceted components, this conversation lays the groundwork for a well-informed decision-making process regarding future living scenarios. This dialogue is a comprehensive conversation that delves into various critical aspects, focusing on priorities, timelines for relocation, destination considerations, and financial implications, including costs and benefits.

The Legal Talk is a crucial conversation that revolves around essential legal documents. It serves as a cornerstone in planning for the future, focusing on decision-making capabilities, health-care preferences, and the distribution of assets. This discussion ensures clarity and understanding regarding powers of attorney (designating trusted individuals to act on one's behalf in legal matters), advance directives (articulating preferences for medical care in unforeseen circumstances), and wills (outlining the distribution of assets, ensuring wishes are legally documented). This conversation is pivotal in ensuring preparedness, clarity, and peace of mind when navigating legal matters and potential future eventualities.

The End-of-Life Talk is a deeply important conversation centered on preparedness, encompassing discussions about completed arrangements, the organization of important documents and belongings, and the articulation of personal preferences. It serves as a crucial step in ensuring that everything necessary has been attended to, including financial, legal, and practical matters. This talk aims to provide clarity on the location of important documents, assets, and personal belongings, streamlining the process for those involved. Furthermore, it offers a platform to express and document one's preferences regarding end-of-life care, funeral arrangements, and any other specific wishes, fostering a sense of control and peace of mind amid an inevitably difficult time.

As you see, there is a lot to cover. No wonder families put these types of conversations on the back burner until faced with an elevated situation and a potential crisis. Additionally, many families are met with pushback from their loved ones, who prefer not to bring up the topics for fear of the changes that may be in front of them, which makes broaching these topics even trickier.

So, where to start? Let's break it down into steps so that this whole situation is simplified.

Step 1

Personal assessment. This is a type of journaling exercise. What is currently happening with your senior loved one, and how is it affecting you and your family? What are you currently handling on behalf of your loved ones? What emotions are you personally dealing with? How are you balancing your loved one's needs with your own needs, your family's needs, and your career? What personal objections are you handling to a potentially changing situation?

Step 2

Pull out the specific pieces that can be supported through the talks. This will help you focus and narrow down specifics. It could look like this:

- I only have time to drop by my loved one's house two times per week. (Expectations Talk)
- Mom's care needs are increasing—I do not want to be responsible for them. (Physical Health Talk)
- I don't know who has the power of attorney (POA). (Legal Talk)

Step 3

Narrow the list of conversation topics to the top one or two. They may all need to be discussed—however, you will get much further faster if you complete these conversations in bite-size pieces. What is the most pressing? Choose which talk to begin with.

Step 4

Attempt to get everyone on the same page. This includes siblings and other involved family members. If you approach your loved one from multiple angles, they will do nothing. In cases like this, there is always someone who thinks things are hunky-dory, and that's whom your loved one will gravitate to.

Step 5

Schedule a time to talk with your loved one. It's very important not to blurt out these types of sensitive talks. Book a time and place, and let your loved one know that you would like to have a conversation about something that has been concerning you (noting in brief what it is). This way they can also prepare themselves.

Step 6

Do the thing. Have the talk. Remain calm and collected. Work through it together, piece by piece. Remember that you are all on the same team. Make sure to listen to your loved one's opinions and help handle objections.

Step 7

Plan to move forward. This is an essential component. If this is not done, then all the awkwardness and this difficult conversation will have most likely been in vain. Conversations without a road map are just words in the wind.

Step 8

Reevaluate often to make sure everything is still going the way you want. It is important to reevaluate and adjust whenever necessary in order to stay on track.

Eldercare conversations, while awkward, have many positive effects. They recognize your loved one's fears and concerns and validate their feelings. There is also value and importance in preplanning and being proactive to avoid crisis-driven decisions. Remember, whether you have the talk or not, a crisis could be just around the corner. Would you prefer to be ready for it or scrambling for answers?

KEY TAKEAWAYS

1. The talks are uncomfortable because they are important.

2. Tackling one talk at a time works best to get things moving.

CHAPTER 5:

ELDERCARE RED FLAGS

When things start to change, it's often slow and without a lot of cause for concern. Whether it is due to denial on the part of the senior or the family member, often care changes go unidentified and are swept under the rug. It is not until these new care concerns begin to compile that any additional thought or action is directed toward them. Unfortunately, in many situations things are left unsaid and unaddressed for so long that they teeter on becoming crisis situations.

This chapter is dedicated to addressing some of the common concerns that come across my desk in conversations with families. The interesting thing is that even when families are describing situations to me, they often still don't understand their significance and the danger their loved ones are in. Instead, families have usually called to "start" looking into things and get some direction. Their current care situation has become normalized to them, but once I hear about it, my spidey-sense starts tingling! Consider if any of these snippets of conversations sound familiar.

SITUATION 1

Daughter: "I am looking for some information about long-term care. My mom isn't on board yet, but my dad has advanced dementia."

Amy: "Has your dad begun to wander or become a flight risk?"

Daughter: "Well, he has gone outside a few times by himself, and we had to go look for him."

Believe it or not, I hear about this type of situation very frequently. Usually, the loved one who has begun to get lost still has all or a lot of their mobility, but dementia has reached a point where the loved one has lost the cognitive ability to remember how to get home. In my experience, something needs to be done right away in cases like this. The solution could be as simple as a GPS alert bracelet or as complex as a full move to a senior living building. Interestingly enough, most people who call me in these situations are not on long-term care waiting lists yet, even though they are calling about long-term care. Having to search for someone with dementia who has gotten lost outside should not have to be a "thing" you do multiple times.

ELDERCARE RED FLAGS

SITUATION 2

[While in a senior's apartment with his daughter]

Amy: "How is making meals and getting groceries going?"

Senior: "Well," *[he laughs]* "it would be better if Martha would stop leaving the stove on! She just hates the microwave."

As dementia advances, many individuals still have decent long-term memory and remember how to cook. However, while in the moment, their short-term memory is not strong enough, and they can become distracted, resulting in an element on the stove being left on.

Please address this right away—for the safety of your loved ones, for their neighbors, and for yourself. Something can go very wrong very quickly when stoves are left on. Even unplugging the stove is a better solution. Other solutions include bringing in meals, having a caregiver come in to meal prep and cook, having the spouse pick up the extra duty, or making a move to a safer environment such as a retirement home.

SITUATION 3

Daughter: "Mom can get around the apartment except when it comes to the sunken living room. She leaves her walker at the top, goes down these three steps, and furniture-walks to the couch."

This can be an easier fix than you might think. Moving the living room or TV up to the top of the stairs in another space or room will eliminate the need for Mom to go down those stairs several times a day and will reduce the risk of falls. This individual was also attempting to go out back to have a cigarette. Setting up a seating area for her to smoke outside the front door, adding a walker at the bottom of the stairs, or adding extra handrails were all solutions for this family, at least for the time being.

SITUATION 4

Is your loved one eating tea and toast for most of their meals?

If so, there may be a nutrition issue to consider. Although tea and toast is an easy meal to prepare and it makes people feel warm and cozy (and a great company name, I might add), if your loved one has gotten to a stage where this is their go-to meal, it's time for a change. Whether you bring in meals, bring in a caregiver to cook, or make a move to a retirement home, this, too, can be easily addressed, as long as it is not left too long.

SITUATION 5

Son: "Mom's network of friends has dwindled, and we don't see her going out anymore."

In situations where your loved one has become more housebound(for a variety of reasons)it is necessary to remain actively involved. Your loved one may not be going out because there is no one to go with, because the weather is bad, or even because of reduced mobility. Isolation is a huge issue for all of us but especially for seniors. Being involved with some sort of activity involving other people stimulates the brain and reduces the effects of isolation and loneliness. Many seniors find themselves in this situation when their spouses pass away. The main stumbling block usually ends up being that the seniors do not know what to do or how to do it. If your loved one is in this situation, help them brainstorm and get actively involved. Again, this is usually an easier fix than you might think, but it all starts with open communication and action.

SITUATION 6

Daughter-in-law: "Dad's care needs seem to be changing, and the home care personal-support worker is unsure how to get Dad involved in more things. She is unable to convince him to have a shower."

This is a situation that should be closely monitored, as there is potential for it to get out of hand quickly. Personal hygiene is a must for all of us. The advice I gave in this situation was to evaluate whether the personal-support worker had the necessary skills to be able to use gentle persuasion techniques to get the showers and care done. If not, the family should either be looking for a different care worker or looking to make a move.

SITUATION 7

Daughter: "Mom and Dad are living in their own home, which is very large with a lot of land. Mom is Dad's caregiver, as he has Parkinson's, but she is beginning to have some short-term memory issues. They are still independent and want to look at senior apartments."

This is an expansion of Anna and Mary's situation from earlier and is a tough situation. An individual with Parkinson's often requires a lot of very scheduled medication. If Mom, who has memory concerns, oversees this medication delivery, both Dad and Mom could be in trouble. Additionally, looking for a senior apartment without services could work for a while, but another move will be in their future, usually sooner rather than later. Consider in this situation the amount of effort the first move will require—the downsizing, setup, and emotional energy that are required to move two individuals with progressive health concerns. To have to turn around and do it again in a short amount of time will be straining on the entire family. It would be much better for the entire family to look at a suite in a retirement home on the more independent, supportive floors. This way, some of the care needs, such as medication distribution, will be taken care of, and if something happens, the parents will have the ability to move within the home, which is much easier than moving buildings. Yet this still gives the parents independence in their living space.

As there are many, many more situations that come up that I address in my work with families. This is just the tip of the iceberg. What is interesting is that many of the situations resemble a common few. If you are in these types of situations, consider talking to someone, whether it is a friend, a neighbor, a coworker, or a professional. You might be surprised to learn that others are also going through—or have gone through—something similar, and they can offer you an added perspective to consider.

KEY TAKEAWAYS

1. Become a detective. Keep your eye on changing situations, and be ready to act.

2. Although the specific situation details may differ, many others are dealing with similar situations, so reach out for support.

PART 2:
PREPLANNING

CHAPTER 6:

LAYING THE FOUNDATION

Carepath Planning

Please note: the following three chapters are written as general guidelines, terms and systems may differ depending on where you live. Throughout North America, these terms and systems should be relatively standard. However, as you will see in the next three chapters, the systems are complicated and have a lot of idiosyncrasies, so it is difficult to nail things down 100% for you here. Please use this book as a guide, and make sure to check with your local coordinators and other professionals.

Throughout the senior-living industry, the term "assisted living" is defined in various ways depending on context. For someone remaining at home and bringing in care, assisted living can perhaps look like companion care or meal prep and housekeeping. In a retirement home, it can mean all of that plus any amount of care that an individual requires. In a long-term care home, assisted living only begins at what I call a medium level of care and does not encompass the more independent tasks such as only requiring meals and medication management. And last, in hospital settings, assisted living is used to refer to the entire senior-housing system, whether your loved one wants to stay at home, move to a retirement home, or go into long-term care.

The senior-living industry uses this blanket terminology so that they can create the opportunity to engage and speak with all sorts of clients, regardless of the care level the client requires. This is also done because most families are unsure of their needs and where they can find help. In the hospital system, more often than not hospital staff are not as familiar with the changing availability in what homes can provide and therefore use the term "assisted living" as a catchall.

Unfortunately, using this unspecific terminology has done little to inform families and has instead ended up confusing them. Additionally, it has set retirement homes and long-term care homes up for failure. Should a home not be able to provide the kind of "assisted living" a family was expecting, they will walk away deterred, more stressed, and confused, often not having a great impression of the home or of the industry at large.

In short, not all senior living is created equal. Retirement homes don't all offer the same level of care and services, and they are different from long-term care homes. Home care services also don't offer the same level of care as each other. When all three avenues use the same terminology interchangeably, it creates a chaotic experience. It's time to clarify things.

So what exactly does the language of Eldercare mean? Let's break it down.

All the following care options can fall under the term "assisted living" (or "ASL") and will be used throughout your Eldercare journey in both the hospital system and the housing system. It's important to have basic knowledge to help you better understand the processes and different avenues. Often, my colleagues and I are asked to consult with hospital-discharge planners as the family feels they do not speak the same language.

INSTRUMENTAL ACTIVITIES OF DAILY LIVING

Instrumental activities of daily living (or IADLs) are tasks learned in our teen years, such as managing transportation, finances, medication, meal preparation, shopping, and general communications. These activities are where we often see families first starting to get more involved. These activities can usually be taken care of while an individual remains in their home, and assistance with these activities doesn't often require a move, although many independent seniors do choose to investigate retirement living as an alternative option when they begin to struggle.

ACTIVITIES OF DAILY LIVING

Activities of daily living (or ADLs) are self-care tasks we learn when we are young, such as walking, bathing, transferring (moving by ourselves from one place to another), toileting, dressing, grooming, and feeding. These, too, can be done in one's home. Additionally, both retirement homes and long-term care homes can take care of these needs.

A note on receiving care while at home—when an individual remains at home and receives care, one needs to really keep an eye on how much care is being brought into the home. Is it enough care or too little? Additionally, as care levels increase, so do personal-support workers' hours, and the bill at the end of the month may start getting more hefty. If it is your loved one's desire to remain at home and receive a lot of care, it might be worth looking into a live-in support worker, as they are often less expensive than hourly support workers. As a comparison, I have seen individuals requiring 24-hour assistance while at home, with monthly care bills upward of $20,000. In a retirement home, that same care could cost between $6,000 and $15,000 depending on one's location. In a long-term care home the cost would often be less.

INDEPENDENT LIVING

Independent living (or IL) is often used to describe a lifestyle. Usually, the senior who is moving to a retirement home in independent living is looking for an environment where some of their daily chores are taken care of. In this context, "assisted living" is used to describe a lifestyle where meals and housekeeping are provided, and no physical or cognitive care is necessary.

INDEPENDENT SUPPORTIVE LIVING

Independent supportive living (or ISL) is offered to seniors who are living independently but require a small amount of help. This can include support with medications, bathing, and laundry, in addition to meal and housekeeping services. Basically, the services that are being provided are more of the scheduled variety. Staff are not waiting for the resident to call or press a pendant to ask for assistance. Homes that have independent supportive floors are great for seniors who only need a small amount of care because they have the opportunity to live on more independent floors and not on full assisted living floors.

Assisted Living Physical Care Levels

There are essentially two types of care profiles that fall under physical care.

One-person and two-person assists are categories of care that retirement homes and long-term care homes use to assess the level of care that a senior needs. Family caregivers also do this type of care. When thinking about whether someone requires this type of care, consider, *Would the activity be completed without the assistance of someone else?*

One-Person Assist

As a rule of thumb, a one-person assist (or 1PA) means that a senior requires one staff member or family caregiver to support them in completing their ADLs. These activities may include helping the senior transfer out of a bed to a walker or wheelchair, getting dressed, and getting to and using the washroom.

Two-Person Assist

A two-person assist (or 2PA) means that the senior requires two staff members, family caregivers, or a mixture of both to assist with tasks. This often happens when the senior is non-weight-bearing or frail. An example of this would be if a senior needed one person on each side of them to support them when getting out of bed.

In conjunction with this, a mechanical lift may also be required. This device is mostly used to move people who are unable to bear weight, either due to excess weight, frailty, or physical-mobility challenges. When a senior in a retirement home requires the use of a lift, they usually also require a two-person assist for staff and resident safety.

In retirement homes, when a senior's care needs increase to a one-person assist and they are living on a supportive floor, the senior is often—but not always—able to stay in their current suite to receive services. However, when a two-person assist is required, individuals usually need to move to assisted living or physical care floors. This all depends on the home and is worth asking representatives about when considering options.

ASSISTED LIVING (PHYSICAL CARE FLOOR)

A physical care floor can also be called an assisted living floor, or AL. (Confusing, right?) These floors are usually reserved for those who require a one- or two-person assist. Additionally, seniors may look at moving to physical care floors if their mobility is limited and they would like to have meals and activities more centralized on the same floor. Most of these floors have their own self-contained dining rooms and lounges.

BREADCRUMBS

MEMORY CARE FLOOR/SECURED FLOOR

Individuals who have any form of dementia or other types of cognitive impairment may find that a memory care floor (or MC) is appropriate. Memory care is a locked, secure floor that is accessed only via a keypad code. Seniors living in memory care are not permitted to leave the floor without supervision.

A special note about this type of floor—it's generally frowned upon in the senior living industry to have a senior live on this floor too early in their diagnosis of dementia. Everyone's dementia progresses differently, and if someone is placed on this floor prematurely, when they still have a good amount of insight into their changing abilities and are more active and social, you will often notice a decline when they are surrounded by others who are more advanced in the disease, less active and less social.[7]

There are three main reasons this type of floor would be needed/required:

1. The person is a flight/wandering risk, meaning they are looking for a way out. This is sometimes also referred to as exit-seeking. This is often the issue when memory begins to fade but the individual is still

---

[7] "Progression," Alzheimer Society of Canada, last updated 2022, https://alzheimer.ca/sites/default/files/documents/Progression-Overview-Alzheimer-Society.pdf.

physically well. Many people are not able to understand why they can't be on their own if they are feeling well physically. When I discuss this with families, I often describe it as their body being physically well enough to go for a walk as they used to, but their mind is no longer able to get them home.
2. The person requires an advanced amount of cuing (reminding), which requires additional specialized staff.
3. The person would benefit from the specialized activity programming offered on the floor as well as the smaller dining room and increased supervision.

GOVERNMENTAL CARE AT HOME

Governmental care is tricky to speak about in a book, as it has a lot of ins and outs. I will cover it here in brief so that you have a basic understanding.

In Canada, the government offers supportive care services that are funded through taxes and available to all residents. This includes access to long-term care homes and access to government-funded home care. There are eligibility criteria and an acceptance process for both, as well as waiting lists.

While individuals are "in the community," meaning in the home or a retirement home, the government care can come in and supplement other care that may be required. If the individual is at home, they can often access other services, including additional care and other professional services. In a retirement home, the care and services are pared back, from the government, as it is expected that the home would provide services and invoice the clients directly.

I most often see government care covering these tasks:

- AM and PM care. AM care is getting the individual up and ready for the day, including help in the bathroom, help getting dressed, and help with sponge bathing. PM care is the reverse of this.
- Bathing assistance. This helps with one to three showers weekly.

This information will come in handy with the below examples.

CARE MODELS IN RETIREMENT LIVING

As mentioned previously, not all retirement homes are created equal. Some homes have a care-packaging system called à la carte, while others prepackage their care.

There are definitely benefits and drawbacks to each type of care. I'll take a minute here to describe each style and to debunk some myths.

À la Carte Care Packaging

"À la carte care packaging" simply means that care services are individually priced, and a personalized package is created for each resident. The director of care gathers information about the senior's care needs and creates a package specialized for them.

Many families believe that if they use this type of care, they will be nickeled-and-dimed. They falsely believe that they will have to pay for every pill that's distributed and every minute of care. In my experience, this is not the norm, although I have seen it in homes here and there. This style of care is set up so that the pricing is wrapped around actual services, not around the time needed or how often services are delivered.

Here is a comparison to help clarify.

Scenario One

This senior requires

- medication distribution,
- two baths a week,
- AM and PM care, and
- escorts to the dining room and activities.

Scenario Two

This senior requires

- medication distribution,
- two baths a week,
- AM and PM care,
- escorts to the dining room and activities,
- transfers out of bed, and
- incontinence care (bladder).

In these two scenarios, the care costs can differ drastically. They will also be affected by whether or not governmental care is coming in to assist. Let's look at the potential cost breakdowns to give you a better understanding.

À la Carte Care Pricing Example

	Scenario One (less care)		Scenario Two (more care)	
Care Requirements	Care Cost Without Government Subsidy	Care Cost with Government Subsidy	Care Cost Without Government Subsidy	Care Cost with Government Subsidy
Medication	$500	$500	$500	$500
Two Baths	$200	$0	$200	$0
AM Care	$300	$0	$300	$0
PM Care	$300	$0	$300	$0
Escorts	$150	$150	$150	$150
Transfers	—	—	$600	$600
Incontinence (Bladder)	—	—	$1,150	$770
Monthly Care Fees	$1,450	$650	$3,200	$2,020
Accommodation & Hospitality Fees	$2,500	$2,500	$2,500	$2,500
Total Monthly Fee	**$3,950**	**$3,150**	**$5,700**	**$4,520**
When Governmental Care Is Used	Savings of $800/month		Savings of $1,180/month	

As you can see, governmental care workers can do tasks such as AM care and bathing, as well as assistance with incontinence. Often, homes will reduce their costs based on what is being supplied by the government. Keep in mind that this changes based on the home and its location.

Seniors who require a small amount of care services often like this type of à la carte care because they're not paying for care they're not receiving. Additionally, seniors with lower budgets also tend to like this kind of care packaging because they can often bring in government-funded care to help offset the cost of some of the services. Then they can top up the services they need from the home. As you can expect, there is a strategy for everything.

Packaged Care

The other care model is called packaged care. This simply means that the home has prepackaged a certain amount of care, which usually includes some of everything, such as AM/PM care, transfers, baths, medication distribution, escorts, and incontinence care.

Let's look again at the chart from before. As you will see, in a packaged-care scenario, the resident is paying the same price regardless of the care they need. You will also notice that having governmental care coming in does not reduce the price in packaged care.

If you recall, the senior in scenario one only needed the first four services (in **bold**), but in this system, they would pay for everything. This may come in handy down the road, when they require an increase in care assistance.

Packaged Care Pricing vs. à la Carte Care Pricing Example

Care Requirements	Scenario One (less care)		Scenario Two (more care)	
	À la Carte (**with** $ from Government)	Packaged (**no** $ from Government)	À la Carte (**with** $ from Government)	Packaged (**no** $ from Government)
Medication	$500	$500	$500	$500
Two Baths	$0	$200	$0	$200
AM Care	$0	$300	$0	$300
PM Care	$0	$300	$0	$300
Escorts	$150	$150	$150	$150
Transfers	—	$600	$600	$600
Incontinence (Bladder)	—	$1,150	$770	$1,150
Monthly Care Fees	$650	$3,200	$2,020	$3,200
Accommodation & Hospitality Fees	$2,500	$2,500	$2,500	$2,500
Total Monthly Fee	$3,150	$5,700	$4,520	$5,700
	Difference of **$2,550**/month		Difference of **$1,180**/month	

This style of care packaging benefits individuals who have a lot of care needs. Everything is included in this kind of packaging, and seniors don't usually need to be worried about any fluctuations. Additionally, others enjoy this type of packaging when they want to pay a consistent amount, both in the present and on an ongoing basis, for budgeting purposes. Although à la carte is based only on the services that a senior needs and doesn't change without a family conference, there is the potential for that care cost to go up and down as it follows the needs of the senior. Package care pricing is always consistent, whether a senior needs more or fewer services. (Note—this excludes extensive services, such as a two-person assist and feeding.)

However, where you will see the added benefits of comparing the two is when the person using à la carte care packaging is also using governmental services. As you can see in scenario one, there is a substantial difference in cost savings for those using governmental services.

Continuum of Care or Aging in Place Model

This is the model in which someone can move into a retirement home, and as their care needs increase, they can remain in the same home. The advantage to this approach is that the person can continue to live in the place they have come to know, with their social connections, rather than having to move to a different residence when their care needs progress.

In some retirement residences, a person receiving an increased level of care would need to move to a different floor. In other homes, there are two different buildings, one designated as independent living and the other designated as assisted living, usually attached by an underground tunnel.

LAYING THE FOUNDATION

Another possibility is living in a building where seniors could receive care in their original suites.

When looking for a full continuum of care, many families who have a loved one with dementia also consider having a secured memory care floor in the home. It's not always necessary that someone will need to move to that type of floor. However, the purpose of looking for the full continuum is to eliminate as many variables as possible that would require someone to move buildings.

A residence that provides the full continuum of care can be a particularly desirable option for couples who want to stay together regardless of their independent health needs, seniors who don't want to make another major move in the near future, or seniors with conditions that traditionally have a rapid decline.

FLO AND ROGER

Flo and her husband Roger were looking to move to a retirement home due to Roger's increasing needs related to his Parkinson's and the associated dementia. Flo, whose physical and cognitive health were good, was Roger's primary caregiver at home.

In this scenario, it was important to consider not only Roger's needs but also Flo's interests. He needed care; she was independent. Additionally, they both needed their separate spaces. As a strategy, we looked at what Roger's needs might be in the upcoming months and years, what Flo would need in a retirement residence to make her feel at home, and options for two separate living spaces.

For this situation, they had three potential solutions:

They could move into an independent apartment in a seniors' residence with a full kitchen so that Flo could still cook and there was better accessibility for Roger, similar to being in an apartment building. For this option, home care for Roger would need to be brought in from outside. Apartments geared toward independent seniors do not usually have care on-site.

They could move into a retirement home that offered independent supportive living in the suite so that Roger and Flo could live together in the same suite and stay together for the longest possible time.

They could move Roger into a studio suite in a retirement home that offered assisted living and move Flo into a studio in the same residence on an independent floor.

LAYING THE FOUNDATION

For Roger and Flo, my recommendation was either option 2, ensuring that they chose a two-bedroom suite, or option 3, moving into two separate suites on different floors but in the same building.

But these decisions are more than just logistics. We also must consider the human factor and look at things holistically.

Flo had mentioned to me that she was really missing her own space where not everything had to do with Parkinson's and reminders of illness. She said that in order to combat this, she always had flowers in the house and kept them in a little corner of her own. Additionally, she hadn't been sleeping well at night—Roger had been getting up at 3 AM to work on projects and often woke her up.

Flo also let me know that Roger had become more dependent, and she hadn't been able to get a single moment to herself. Flo told me, "Amy, sometimes I just want to sit down for half an hour and watch the news. I don't want to be interrupted, and I don't want to have to get up to get something for someone."

This last statement really hit home for me as a wife and mother! In fact, on the very day I spoke with

Flo, I had just that morning been sitting on the couch. All I had wanted to do was drink my coffee in peace, and instead, I had found myself juggling requests for juice, advice, and head scratches from my daughter, husband, and dog. Everyone was fighting for my attention and wanting me to do something for them. All I wanted to do was have an uninterrupted moment to myself.

Option 3 offered Roger the care he needed and Flo the independence she wanted, but it also gave Flo the opportunity to be with Roger as often as she liked, for meals and visits and outings. Option 3 not only supported Flo so that she could have her flowers and watch the news by herself when she wanted to, but it also gave her the independence and freedom of doing things by herself or going out with friends and family from time to time, knowing that Roger was safe and well cared for.

When two people—one needing care and one independent—are looking to make a move to retirement living, it's important to find a healthy and compassionate balance. Looking at the situation holistically allows you to do this.

LAYING THE FOUNDATION

> In this situation, I needed to help Flo and Roger choose a home that didn't have a setting that felt like "too much care," because it's important that the independent person doesn't feel out of place. However, you also need to ensure that the home you choose has the ability and capacity to provide as much care as your loved ones needs or wants added in the future so that the partner needing assistance is taken care of properly throughout their stay.

A professional skilled in navigating the senior-housing industry can help you with these advanced strategies.

As an additional note, Flo and Roger would not have been able to accomplish this type of living scenario in a long-term care home. More on long-term care in chapter 8.

Beyond the care wording and definitions, there can be a lot to know about seniors' housing. The average person probably wouldn't consider that there are strategies—sometimes advanced ones—that should be looked at when navigating the housing industry. Just like when buying a new home, there is a best season and location when considering senior living. You then need to consider present and future care needs as well as emotions. The search is a full-time job.

KEY TAKEAWAYS

1. Care terminology is confusing. Knowing the care goals will help you navigate the senior-living terrain.

2. Governmental home care may be available. Make sure to inquire to see if your loved one qualifies.

CHAPTER 7:

UNDERSTANDING THE RETIREMENT LIVING INDUSTRY

The number one question that families ask when beginning their senior-living search is "What is the difference between a retirement home and a long-term care home?"

There is a huge amount of confusion out there around the process and costs associated with applying for, qualifying for, and moving into a retirement home vs. a long-term care home.

When looking to make a move, there are many variables that need to be considered. The very first step is to make sure you understand the terminology. Next, it's important to understand the difference between the two types of homes. I will cover retirement homes in this chapter and long-term care homes in the following chapter.

RETIREMENT HOMES

A retirement home is a privately run facility where seniors pay out of pocket to live. Retirement homes are also called assisted living homes and retirement residences or communities. Generally speaking, retirement homes are not government funded, and there are usually no substantial financial subsidies available to support people wanting to live in retirement homes. There are, however, a few tax credits that may assist. Be sure to check with your tax agency for more details.

Retirement homes are what I call a social model. In a retirement home, a senior has access to meal and housekeeping services. There is also a full calendar of social activities to partake in. Retirement homes are communal settings where residents share a large dining room and social rooms. In this type of community, a senior would have their own suite/apartment with a private bathroom.

Seniors choose to move to a retirement home for a number of reasons, including the following:

1. They are at risk of social isolation, either because their social network has dwindled over time or because their physical or cognitive needs inhibit them from remaining social.

2. Maintaining a nutritious diet is difficult for them because of the physical challenges of shopping and meal preparation.
3. Their home is not appropriately set up for them to age in place—for example, it may be too large or have a lot of stairs.
4. Home maintenance and upkeep have become too much.
5. It's no longer safe for them to remain at home due to a dementia diagnosis.
6. It's no longer safe for them to remain at home due to their physical needs.
7. Their spouse requires care that they can no longer handle on their own.
8. They wish to receive care in any amount.

Many times, people consider moving to a retirement home because they have lost their partner and have become isolated. Often, people who are isolated in their later years have some sort of mobility or cognitive condition that limits where and when they can go out to socialize. Retirement homes can easily provide much-needed opportunities to be with others in the same peer group and with similar interests.

MAGGIE

Maggie came to me looking for a community that had an active social calendar and a bit of a night life. Her daughter was concerned because Maggie loved to be social, but getting out was difficult for her, and the apartment building she lived in was full of government workers with very few seniors. Maggie had made an effort to get involved in her new place, but with the sheer lack of people and activities, it had been a pretty quiet and lonely existence. Maggie was the perfect candidate for a retirement home.

To function in a healthy way and carry out ADLs such as meal preparation, shopping, and medication management, a person needs an adequate combination of motor skills and cognitive abilities. For this reason, some seniors choose to make the move to retirement living to lift the stress of these activities. Sometimes, it's a family member who encourages the move because they are concerned about potential (or actual) mistakes made by their loved one in nutrition and medication management. Mistakes in these key areas can have significant consequences.

As for care levels, some retirement homes have the ability and capacity to provide the same level of care as long-term care homes. However, this does vary by residence and by city, and of course, budget is always a factor as well.

I spoke about this earlier, but to add to my note about couples and care in retirement living, many choose to move to a retirement home setting in order to remain together longer. In doing this, they can access different levels of care and often remain in the same building, if not the same suite.

An alternative to moving directly into a retirement home permanently is to try a winter respite or a short respite stay. A winter respite is generally three to four months long, and essentially, a senior signs a contract with the understanding that, after a set time, they will be leaving. Many people enjoy winter respite stays, and if they decide to stay after the allotted time, they already have a signed agreement. A short respite stay, also known as a convalescent stay, is, in contrast, a short stay usually ranging from two weeks to two months and can be used for a variety of reasons including caregiver reprieve, vacation, or recovery after surgery.

Additionally, many individuals also choose to live in retirement homes while they are on waiting lists for long-term care homes. More about this in chapter 8.

SELECTING A RETIREMENT HOME

Your loved one has finally come to the decision to make a move to a retirement home or, at the very least, is considering the options and is willing to do some research. Congrats! As a professional, I can tell you that this is a very hard decision for many people to get to, and now that you've arrived, you want to make this as simple as possible. Often, when things become more complicated and stressful, people tend not to want to move forward. The idea here is to come to a decision as accurately as possible with the least amount of stress.

But how do you do that? In all honesty—and I know I'm biased—working with a professional is your best option to make sure you consider all the available options based on your needs and goals. Look for a professional who can work with all the retirement homes in your area and narrow them down to the best fit, providing you with an apples-to-apples comparison.

Short of that, here are some of my top tips that will help you narrow down retirement home options.

1. Know the budget. Having a good understanding of how much money is available to put toward the new retirement home will help to not only narrow down the search but also to know how much of a budget is available for care down the road. Please know that retirement living has a huge range of cost and often is dependent on the size of the suite and the amount of care required. If the budget is $2,500 or lower, consider that the timing of a move will make a lot of difference. I speak more about this in chapter 9. Download our retirement home budget planner to

begin putting things together. It is linked at the end of the book.
2. Next, narrow down the location to something that works great for you/your loved one and for any other family members and friends who need to have easy access. Most people try to stay near the neighborhoods that they are familiar with. Alternatively, some choose to move to another city to be closer to their families.
3. Consider what type of care is needed now and what it might look like in the future so that you can better evaluate the home's ability to care for your loved one.
4. Ask the questions. At the end of the book, I've included a link to a download of comparables that you can use to compare retirement homes side-by-side.

MOVE-IN PROCESS

It's quite simple, actually. Once the home is chosen, a deposit or signed reservation form is necessary to hold the suite. There is some required paperwork to sign, and the home will collect some personal medical information from the resident as well as their family doctor. From there, some of the next steps include choosing the move date, booking the elevator and moving professionals, and setting up the suite. Don't forget: retirement homes require tenant insurance.

WHAT IF IT'S NOT A RIGHT FIT?

Many individuals and families find themselves choosing a retirement home but learning sooner or later that it's not the best fit. Sometimes a home is a great fit in the beginning, but things change in the home (such as management or staffing), or care needs increase and surpass what the home can provide. Once this has happened, there are usually two options.

1. Research and move to another retirement home
2. Wait it out for a move to long-term care

The latter is of particular interest if the care needs have surpassed what the home is able to provide. In this case, it would be wise to connect with your government care coordinator to see if there is more care they can bring in or to see if the resident can be placed on the crisis list and moved to a long-term care home sooner. More on this in the next section.

Most retirement homes require 30 days' notice. Sometimes it's possible to waive that notice if moving within the same brand of homes.

IS THERE A WAITING LIST FOR RETIREMENT HOMES?

Waiting lists have now become the norm, especially when looking for an assisted living or memory care floor. I talked about this at the beginning of the book, but due to the COVID years, the aging of the baby boomer demographic, and the regular flow of moves that happen in retirement living, waiting lists have begun getting longer. Additionally, larger suites, such as two bedrooms, have often had waiting lists in the past, as there are very few available and independent couples usually occupy them for many years.

If there is the ability and desire to move to a retirement home while still independent, then the senior will have first choice of an internal move when their care needs change.

ISN'T A RETIREMENT HOME EXPENSIVE?

It can be.

It all comes down to square footage [the larger the suite, the more expensive it is] how much care is needed (the more care the home needs to provide, the higher the cost), and the location of the home in the city. The range of costs varies significantly from city to city, home to home, and between independent living and full assisted living.

I know, I know—so how much are we looking at, you ask?

The truth is that prices vary. You may have noticed that retirement residences don't list their prices on their websites. That's because pricing is subjective and depends on many factors.

BREADCRUMBS

At the time of this publishing, for an independent resident living in a studio (bachelor apartment–type) suite in Ottawa, Canada, pricing can start around $3,000 per month. However, you can expect up to $4,500. This price typically includes the suite rental, meals and snacks, weekly housekeeping, and laundering of linens and towels.

RED FLAGS TO LOOK FOR IN A RETIREMENT RESIDENCE

When people are new to something, it can be difficult to know if some thing is average or out of the norm. Not knowing what to expect not only makes people uneasy and scared, but it also has the potential to set someone up for failure if things are dismissed as normal when they are not. To assist you and your loved one in the retirement home search, I have listed a few things to watch out for while touring

1. **The home tells you that they can do all care up to and including palliative or that they have a full continuum of care, so a second move will not be necessary.**
   This could be correct, but it may depend on other circumstances. If the home cannot do a two-person assist or provide memory care, and you believe that one or both of those things may be required in the future, a future move might be necessary. Consider any progressive-care concerns, including any condition

that attacks the body, such as Parkinson's or multiple sclerosis, as well as conditions of the mind, like dementia. Often, though not always, these types of conditions require a lot more care as time goes on, and if you do not want another move to happen in the future, you might be better off making sure the home can accommodate this care.

2. **The home has been recently purchased.**

    New ownership usually comes with a lot of upheaval. Sometimes the quality goes down, and the staff and residents are left unsettled. It may not stay this way, but then again, it may. Make sure to ask the home about the change and if they foresee any large changes. Additionally, you can also ask residents and family members while on tour.

    On the flip side, a change in ownership could be just what the home needed and may be a very positive experience for everyone.

3. **Staffing is unstable and ever changing.**

    If the home doesn't have any long-serving staff, or if staff start to leave, there is an issue, usually with management either on a home level or at a higher level. You should inquire to find out more information before deciding whether that home is the right fit. This is especially true with care staff if your loved one is in need of care support from the home.

4. **The home is not compliant with regulations.**
   If the home is in a location that has a regulatory authority overseeing retirement residences, citations may be available online. Steer clear of homes that are not taking care of their citations, take a long time clearing them up, or have citations that go against your ethics.

Depending on where you are located, retirement homes can definitely vary in aesthetics, care services, and food service, and regulations. Some locations do not have regulations for private retirement homes at all. Senior housing can be a complicated process to navigate, and finding information on the internet is still quite limited in this industry.

KEY TAKEAWAYS

1. Retirement homes are a great option for a variety of reasons, and seniors don't need to wait until care is required to make a move to a more relaxed lifestyle.

2. Make sure to have discussions about retirement homes with a local professional. Retirement homes are not all created equal, it's up to families to do their due diligence.

CHAPTER 8:

UNDERSTANDING THE LONG-TERM CARE INDUSTRY

A long-term care home is a publicly subsidized seniors' residence. I often refer to them as a medical model. These homes are run by private companies, not-for-profit organizations, cities, and municipalities. Seniors move to these types of homes due to care needs when they don't have access to or have maxed out on available services in the community.

Long-term care homes require a special type of road map to navigate. You can't pop into a local home to sign up when you are ready. There are processes, and yes, unfortunately there are waiting lists. Bottom line—you need to plan for this type of move.

These are the general steps to obtain access to a long-term care home:

1. Evaluate your loved one's care needs. Do you or your loved one feel that care needs are increasing and are getting more difficult to handle? If so…

2. Contact the local government health agency and ask for a long-term care assessment.
3. Once qualified, paperwork, including submitting top choices of long-term care homes will need to be submitted.
4. The homes will approve or deny the application. If approved, your loved one will be placed on waiting list(s). An applicant can be on more than one list at the same time.
5. Until there is a bed available, your loved one will remain in the community with support as needed.

The strategy for moving into a long-term care home is just that: a strategy! You should first consider which stage your loved one is at. The three common stages include the following:

1. Your loved one already has high care needs.
2. They are in need of some basic assistance with care
3. They are completely independent.

1. YOUR LOVED ONE ALREADY HAS HIGH CARE NEEDS

If you are in this situation, you will most likely need to find a solution for your loved one's care needs for the short term until they are accepted into a long-term care home.

UNDERSTANDING THE LONG-TERM CARE INDUSTRY

There are a few options:

- Ask family and friends for assistance.
- Engage a private agency to come in to the home to provide care (known as family-funded home care).
- Receive care from the government-funded agency (for example, personal-support workers, which is another form of home care).
- Move into a retirement home while on the waiting list.

Being put on a crisis-placement list may be an option. In this situation, care needs are assessed against predetermined criteria, and if your loved one's care needs are high enough, the application is moved to the crisis waiting list of the homes that you have already applied to. In order to qualify in this circumstance, the case coordinator must see that the care needs can no longer be taken care of in the community and that there are no other reasonable options. This type of move is not immediate, however, and can still involve a bit of a waiting time that varies from home to home. In some locations, there are no crisis-placement lists, and seniors instead need to go to the hospital and accept the next open bed. Locations with crisis-placement lists may have an open-bed policy as well, but the crisis list is a step in between.

Most of the moves to long-term care homes happen from "community," meaning from one's home. This includes any place a senior may be physically living: at their home, with a family member, or in a retirement home.

Many people still believe that they can be admitted into a long-term care home directly from the hospital. Although this does happen, it's not the preferred method, and it is not as likely as it was in the old days. The system is simply too overcrowded. Additionally, if your loved one is being placed in a long-term care home from the hospital, it will most likely not be their top choice.

2. THEY ARE IN NEED OF SOME BASIC ASSISTANCE WITH CARE,

This is probably the best time to start looking at long-term care homes if moving to one is an option your family would like to have in the future. In this situation, the senior can cope but needs some assistance such as help with medication, dressing, bathing, and maybe meals and housework. These needs can usually easily be taken care of in the community—either at home or in a retirement home—and may not require going to a long-term care home right away. In this situation, depending on the care needs, the senior may or may not be qualified for a long-term care home. It'll come down to the assessment.

3. THEY ARE COMPLETELY INDEPENDENT

This is a tricky spot to be in. I always appreciate and commend planning! However, the strategy is a little different when it comes to dealing with independent seniors. In this case, I would recommend learning about the system (see step 2 below), touring/choosing preferred long-term care homes, and then waiting until a time when your loved one starts needing more care and can envision making the move. At that point, they can add their name to the waiting lists once they qualify.

Unfortunately, the Western health-care system is set up to be reactive and not proactive, meaning that if a person doesn't require care, they can't get on the waiting list prematurely. Doing your research early, at the very least, prepares you to make selections quickly when the time comes.

The strategy for choosing long-term care homes should include the following:

- Deciding how long of a waiting list is acceptable
- Determining location preferences
- Touring the homes[8]
- Contacting the assigned coordinator and letting them know which homes have been selected

---

8 Homes often only tour on select days and times, and sometimes there are a few weeks between when you originally place your call and when you tour.

If your loved one is selected to move into a long-term care home, they'll need to make the decision *and* move in a matter of days. The home will not hold a suite for them. In fact, should they decline the bed, most often, they will be removed from the list completely and be unable to reapply for multiple months. When they feel ready to begin the qualifying process a second time, they will be placed at the bottom of the lists again. This process varies depending on where you are located.

If your loved one needs services at home or in a retirement home at any point in this process, or even before that, you can speak to the governmental care coordinator about getting government-funded assistance, look into a private home care company, or use the services at the retirement home.

VIC

When Vic got in touch with me, he had just returned to his home from the hospital and felt that he needed more support and social interaction than he had before going into the hospital. Vic was worried that if he moved into a retirement residence, he would lose his place on the waiting list for a long-term care home. I reassured him that he could live in a retirement home *and* stay on the list.

> Once he was able to get past this objection, he chose to move to a retirement residence and wait for his spot on the waiting list to come up at the long-term care home.

CRISIS PLACEMENT

In Vic's situation above, one additional circumstance I feel worth bringing to your attention would be if Vic was also on the crisis waiting list. As stated above, just being on the long-term care list does not usually limit your loved one from moving within the community, and remaining on the waiting list. However, should Vic have come to me and told me that he was on the crisis waiting list, I may have given him completely different advice.

Being accepted onto the crisis list means the care coordinator deemed the situation unsafe and that the care needs cannot be met with any combination of caregiving in the home or community. Should a senior then move to a retirement home, as an example, where they *can* meet the senior's care needs, the senior might be taken off the crisis list and only remain on the main long-term care waiting list. It's important to know all the moving pieces and how they fit together.

I have seen this situation a handful of times with families where we needed to make sure there was a strategy to either remain on the crisis list or be in a position to get on the crisis list. The number of hoops families need to jump through in order to get care can be quite wild.

Finally, if your loved one is in a crisis situation and accepted onto the crisis waiting list, they will most likely be asked to add additional homes with shorter waiting lists to their home selections. The crisis waiting lists are per home—there isn't a single list that covers all the homes. Should they be offered their third choice, for instance, and opt to move in there, they can usually remain on the list for their first choice and make a move once it becomes available.

HOSPITAL DISCHARGE AND SENIOR LIVING

Navigating the hospital environment can be challenging for families. They often find themselves in heightened emotional states, piecing together information about their loved ones' conditions while grappling with medical jargon. In many cases, individuals are discharged to senior living communities, especially if returning home poses risks. However, a significant issue arises in the disconnect between the public and private health-care systems. This divide creates barriers for families seeking assistance in the private sector, such as retirement living, when public long-term care homes are at capacity and returning home isn't a feasible option.

UNDERSTANDING THE LONG-TERM CARE INDUSTRY

When families explore retirement living options from the hospital, they will encounter hurdles. Discharge planners are usually unable to offer recommendations and are unfamiliar with the intricacies of the private-housing system, requiring families to possess comprehensive knowledge of the system in a short amount of time. One major reason for this gap is the challenge faced by retirement homes and Eldercare advisors in providing education and support to discharge planners and hospitals due to bureaucratic obstacles. Consequently, patients and families are also unable to easily access this information through the discharge process.

CAN MY LOVED ONE MOVE FROM ONE CITY TO ANOTHER WHEN THEY'RE IN LONG-TERM CARE?

Yes.

If your loved one needs to relocate to another city, and they are not yet officially on the list for long-term care, they may want to wait until they move to save some frustration (if the move is upcoming). When they arrive in the new city, they will be able to apply to the local agency.

If your loved one would like to be moved from one long-term care home to another, that is possible as well. You or your loved one would contact the local agency case coordinator, and they could help with the transfer of information. Keep in mind that if your loved one is switching provinces in Canada, they will need a valid new health card.

BENEFITS AND DRAWBACKS OF LIVING IN A LONG-TERM CARE HOME VS. A RETIREMENT HOME

Affordability and Care

Living in long-term care costs less than living in a retirement home due to the government subsidy. Once room style is decided on, a private or semiprivate room, everything else is taken care of for costs. Your care, lodging, and meals are included, as well as everyday staples such as incontinence products, toilet paper, and soap. This makes budgeting very easy. Additionally, if money runs out, staying in the home may be further subsidized by the government.

Alternatively, in a retirement home you will be paying for the square footage and the care that is needed. The more square feet and care required, the higher the cost. Generally speaking, meals, recreation programming, and housekeeping are included in the suite rate. In most places, but not all, you need to provide all personal products. These are questions to ask when you are investigating options for retirement homes with your loved one.

Couples

Keeping a couple together from the beginning of a move into long-term care is usually not possible, and reuniting them later can be a long process.

In the current Canadian system, both partners need to be assessed and qualify for the long-term care home list independently. Once this is done, it is likely that one partner will move into a home first. The reunification process can be long and tricky. There are no guarantees that the couple will ever end up living together again.

Many couples choose retirement living for this reason. In this situation, they are able to access the care they require while also remaining together.

Ambiance

Long-term care homes are known to have a setting that is more comparable to a hospital setting. Some people who have higher care needs feel more comfortable in this type of setting, as it resembles what they feel they need when it comes to care.

In contrast, retirement homes are more of a social model and are often referred to as cruise ships on land. They appeal to individuals in different ways. Some enjoy homes that feel homey and comfortable, while others enjoy homes with all the bells and whistles.

All in all, the process to access long-term care can be challenging and does require some information gathering. As with many other government programs, there is a lot of red tape, and there are many hoops to jump through. Try to arm yourself with as much information as possible to make the best decisions you can.

> **KEY TAKEAWAYS**
>
> 1. The process to get into long-term care can be long and usually requires individuals to supplement care while waiting.
>
> 2. There are a lot of variables and pieces in the long-term care process. Advocacy and research will be your best friends.

CHAPTER 9

REMAINING IN THE COMMUNITY SAFELY

Strategies for Success

It is very common to come across seniors and their family members who feel as though the best solution when requiring care is to remain at home for as long as possible. Although this can work for a period, depending on circumstances, these same people can turn into the group who insist "I'm going out of this house feet-first". Unfortunately, many of these folks don't actually make a plan to remain safely at home. Picture an ostrich with its head in the sand. Remaining at home safely takes a strategy.

On a high level, when your loved one remains at home, you should be considering at the very minimum how they will continue to live safely, what improvements you will make or need to make for future success, how they will have access to groceries should something happen to you, how they will avoid social isolation, and how they will keep up with things in the house, including but not limited to meal prep, cleaning, and home maintenance. Taking things one step further, consider what their choices will be if remaining at home is no longer an option.

In this chapter, I am going to lay out some strategies for common situations I help families through. Should your loved one be in any of these situations, my hope is that you will be able to take pieces of these strategies into consideration.

HOME CARE STRATEGY

There are three main scenarios that fall under this section: nonmedical, private medical, and government-run medical home care.

Nonmedical Home Care

This type of care usually includes companionship, dressing and bathing, meal preparation, housekeeping, medication reminders, and accompaniment to appointments and outings. These services are offered by the government and companies who assist with medical home care, as well as nonmedical home care companies.

Private Medical Home Care

Medical home care is usually overseen by a nurse and often requires a nurse to assist in some of the activities, including wound care, administering medications, injections, and catheter care. Additionally, personal-support workers can assist with bathing and dressing, transfers, and other ADLs. It is important that these companies have the proper insurance in place, as they are handling medical aspects of home care. The advantage of hiring private home care is that there are no limits on the amount of care a client can receive. However, there is usually a minimum number of hours per visit—somewhere around three—and of course, it's also private pay. You can expect to pay between $25 to $40 an hour on average, depending on the service.

Government-Run Medical Home Care

Government-run medical home care, also known as public medical home care, is very similar to private. However, it is run by the government body and has limits on access and the amount of care received. Individuals must qualify and be accepted in order to obtain this style of home care. Additionally, there is a maximum number of hours allotted weekly, and there's usually a waiting list.

The strategy that many people use is, if they are eligible, to get as much government-run care as possible and supplement it with family caregiving and private home care. The drawbacks to using only public home care are that, due to the system being overloaded, there isn't enough care hours for individuals to adequately cover their needs, there aren't enough hours for individuals, the support workers can be unreliable, and the government don't provide all the services that private home care can provide, like transportation. The ideal would be to combine care sources. However, I have seen some families do this, and especially when there are high care needs, managing the care schedule of who is coming in to do what and when can be a part-time job. For this reason, those whose budgets allow them to hire only private home care usually find it to be a more stable solution.

SERVICES AND RENOVATIONS WHEN REMAINING AT HOME

There are additional items to take into account when choosing to remain at home. It is imperative to make sure that safety is your top priority. Services to inquire about could include these:

- Renovations, both larger-scale (bathrooms, etc.) or smaller renos (grab bars, ramps, etc.).

- Meals, like services for obtaining groceries and meal prep.
- Housekeeping, including cleaning of kitchens, bathrooms, and floors.
- Outdoor maintenance, such as lawn care, snow removal, etc.
- Personal services, including foot care, dental, pet care, etc.
- Emergency pendants and alarms, whether wearables, motion sensors, or door sensors.

In the next few sections, I will go over some very specific strategies that I have used to assist families in the community. These examples are here to help you start thinking about the different types of strategies that may be needed if your loved one is in one of these situations.

STRATEGY FOR SINGLE SENIORS

As life changes, many seniors find themselves in the difficult position of losing their spouse/partner. And for those with no family as well, or those with family who live at a distance, knowing what and when to do things in our elder years can be challenging. Very often, these seniors find themselves in crisis situations because they didn't plan effectively or didn't take steps to ensure they cared for themselves as they aged.

For single seniors, planning is crucial. It's important to recognize that single seniors do not have a partner living in the home with them. If they experience a fall or other health crisis, it will be less likely that they will get immediate help. Ensuring a safe environment is not only vital for their personal well-being but also for the peace of mind of family members who care about their safety.

The other aspect to be concerned about is social isolation. As people get older, especially if they were already introverted, it takes great effort for them to continually reach out and remain involved in activities and social interactions. However, without these efforts, they may find themselves failing not only physically but also mentally.

If your loved one is a single senior, make a plan that includes what will happen in case of emergency, and find ways for them to remain involved in the community. To help you along the way, I have included a link to our estate planner at the end of this book.

STRATEGY FOR LOW-INCOME, HIGH-CARE SENIORS

This scenario is something I see a lot, and honestly, it's going to become more common as pensions dwindle and people don't take steps to secure their safety and incomes. For some, having a low income is a by-product of being a stay-at-home parent and losing the partner who brought in the income. In many cases, having a low income cannot be helped. What can be helped, however, is—you guessed it—planning.

If your loved one is a low-income senior, you need to do everything you can to make sure their home is safe, that they are involved in the community, and that they have tapped into "free" health care, such as home care and other community agencies. Most times, these seniors will not be able to remain in their homes indefinitely. It is a must to know the options in long-term care. When care needs start to increase, please reach out to the governmental care agency and inquire about home care and long-term care. Remember, there are waiting lists, and no one knows when a senior's situation will worsen.

STRATEGY FOR YOUNG SENIORS WITH HIGH CARE NEEDS

To put it simply, our system is just not set up to care for younger seniors. The same public and private home care and long-term care exist for them. However, there is a different strategy when looking for retirement living.

For many, it is difficult to be a 60-year-old living in a retirement home with 85-year-olds. Peer-to-peer connection isn't really there, and many feel a bit like outcasts. The best strategy I have here is in retirement home selection. Choosing a home that is newer or has a younger vibe usually works best which can mean a mixed proportion of high, medium and low care needs. Additionally, some retirement home operators have an age minimum of 65 in order to keep the balance in the home, as their main clientele are seniors. A professional can definitely help here to narrow down selections.

STRATEGY FOR BLENDING CARE NEEDS OF COUPLES

We discussed this a bit earlier. However, I thought it was worth a mention in this section as well, mainly because what I often see is the more independent seniors caring for their partners. This as a whole isn't unusual, but neither is the fact that these caregivers often burn themselves out and don't know when to throw in the towel, whether it is to bring in home care or family support or to move one or both of the pair.

If you or the caregiving senior is seeing this happen, accessing governmental home care will be essential, whether or not you or your loved one can physically do the care on your /their own. This can look like physical care for your loved one or respite for you.

RUTH AND ROBERT

Ruth's daughter called me in to do an Eldercare strategy session with her parents. Ruth was an independent senior caring for her husband, Robert, who had advanced dementia. Ruth took care of everything in the home, including groceries and meal prep, and assisted Robert with showers and appointments. Things were starting to pile up for the family, and Mom was in denial. Every solution I offered her resulted in her saying, "I can do that." It took our whole time together for Ruth to start coming to terms with their situation.

In these situations, it's not overly important whether you *can* do the care—what matters is whether doing the increasing amount of care will put you in danger. Ruth was doing everything because she couldn't let go of the control, so much so that she was putting herself in danger.

In situations like this, you need to bring in support early and often. As the caregiver, try to remove the ego and get in as much help as you can. You won't see caregiver burnout coming until it is already upon you. The strategy here is to get the care routine in early so that your loved one can remain safely in the home for as long as they want. The alternative is that you burn out, and there is no one to care for your loved one, resulting in all sorts of crises where you won't have a choice but to rely on the people you didn't want to rely on in the first place, except in a more involved and more intense way.

BREADCRUMBS

STRATEGY FOR FAMILIES LIVING TOGETHER

Families living together can take on many forms. The world is full of diverse living situations, and every situation includes a fresh set of family dynamics—therefore, looking at each situation separately and holistically is essential. Families can be tight knit or distant. The situation can be complicated by illness or physical limitations. And, in some cases, seniors could still be caring for their children or grandchildren in their home.

So what about the option of having Mom or Dad—or both—live with their adult children?

MARK

Mark and his family chose to have Mom move into their home instead of having her go to a retirement home. As time passed, the family found that caring for their mom's changing needs was difficult and time consuming. Privacy was at an all-time minimum, and stress was starting to compound.

Mark's situation is very common. Often, families bring their loved ones to live with them because they think it would be great to have Mom and/or Dad around, safe, close by, and away from their own home, where they may have been in danger or at risk. Sometimes, that turns out okay.

However, most times we see this situation taking a huge emotional and physical toll on families. Roles change, and the extra burden of being a taxi driver, pharmacist, social convener, chef, and emergency responder can be exhausting. Many of the adult children in these situations have families of their own also living with them, which adds another layer of complexity and stress.

Not long ago, I worked with a couple who originally had their mom living with them, but with her increasing care needs, it was becoming too much for them to handle. They ended up hiring private home care to provide care for their mother in their home. The problem they were facing was the responsibility of caring for Mom while dealing with a huge amount of guilt for having to work at the same time under the same roof. Their guilt stemmed from *them* not being the primary caregivers during the day.

I found that I really connected with this situation—again, because of what was going on in my own life.

When my daughter was a newborn, her dad took paternity leave, and I continued to work. I worked full-time from my home office and in the community. I remember more than once creeping up the back stairs, trying not to be heard or seen so that I could get some work done. I was torn, pulled between the obligation to work and the guilt of not being able to spend time with my family. I faced struggles with my home being both a place of business and a place of care simultaneously. It can be difficult for the one being cared for to understand that "these are my work hours, I'll be available later," and for them to *pretend* that you're not there.

When moving a loved one in with the family is being considered, I caution people to have a hard and honest look at the plan for the present, as well as the plan for down the road. The goal is to make the transition as smooth as possible. It's crucial to put strategies in place and be ready to modify the plan as needed. There are often things, medically and otherwise, that have been hidden, and they sometimes present themselves after the move, which can add extra pressure. Ask the questions in advance, and be ready to act on the answers.

Remember, too, that moving is tough and change is difficult for people of all ages. Having a senior parent move in with family, only to be potentially moved out again, can be especially stressful for everyone. It might be worth considering whether one single move is the best option. This is especially true when an individual has dementia. Multiple moves often result in additional confusion that in time may settle, but often not completely.

REMAINING IN THE COMMUNITY SAFELY

MAVIS

After a fall and a short stint in the hospital, Mavis was looking to make a move to a retirement home to recover for six weeks. She was newly in a wheelchair, and her son had taken it upon himself to renovate his entire home so that she could come back and live with him. At her young age of 95, this is what Mavis wanted too.

When I hear these stories, which is more often than you would think, it's hard not to offer advice to the family members. Most of the time, the question I want to ask is "To what end?" Don't get me wrong, I think it is amazing that these adult children have so much love for their parents that they are willing to spend sometimes hundreds of thousands of dollars to equip the home. But there may be drawbacks. And is moving your loved one into your home truly the best approach?

If you are in this situation, please consider this: Your loved one may only be able to live in the home for a very short time. In a case like this, all the renovations you have done will be wasted money and time that could have been spent in other ways. Also, you and your family will have to continue living in a home that was purpose built and renovated for someone else's needs. In situations like this, even the resale value of your home may be affected.

It's also worth considering that even with all the renovations, your home still might not be the best and safest place for your senior loved one to live in. It also may not be the best living situation for their social needs. As a family caregiver, you may not always be able to hang out with your loved one. Many adult children have a lot of guilt around this and tell me, "My mom is just watching TV all day."

Many times, seniors with complex and complicated care needs may need to move to long-term care, as getting a system together in the home can be challenging. Additionally, Canadian life expectancy is approximately 81 years.[9] In Mavis's case, she was already 95.

I think more things need to be considered in a situation like this, over and above "I want my mom to live with me," or "My loved one doesn't want to move out of their home and will do whatever it takes to stay." Be sure to take the time to consider all aspects and talk things through before jumping in. These are times when an outside voice of reason may be of assistance to share a perspective from a more distant viewpoint. It can be helpful to consult with someone who is not as close to the situation, such as a real estate agent, health-care professional, or housing professional.

---

9 "Life Expectancy."

STRATEGY FOR SENIORS CARING FOR ADULT CHILDREN

Once in a while, I'll work with a senior couple who is still caring for their adult child at home. Usually the child has some form of illness or chronic condition. The parents have always been their child's caregivers and are hesitant to move or change things, even though they themselves may now require help.

You may be surprised to know that some retirement homes allow these adult children to move in with their parents. In my experience, this has worked out to be a good and viable solution, as everyone gets the care they need, and if the seniors were to pass away, the adult child would still be cared for by the home.

BERT AND JANE

With the thought of moving into a retirement home on their mind, Bert and Jane were unsure of how they would do it. Their son, who had multiple sclerosis, had lived with them for the past few years as his multiple sclerosis started to worsen. It was important for Bert, Jane, and their son that they remain living together as a family, but now they needed more care and a new plan. With work and "stuff" piling up in their home, the family would have found themselves in a crisis situation if they had stayed at home much longer.

This is just one of many situations that I typically run into. I've seen similar scenarios, too, when a parent passes away and the remaining partner, who also has care needs, is left to take on the responsibility of caring for their child on their own.

As I've said, it may come as a pleasant surprise that a retirement home could or would accommodate a whole family. Thankfully, the retirement home industry is changing and is open to interpretation and individualization. I have also seen sisters and friends move in together.

My best advice—if you are unfamiliar with the industry or unsure of what's out there, it's always worth checking with a professional when designing your strategy and exploring your options. You never know unless you ask.

STRATEGY FOR WHEN AND WHERE TO MOVE

Given the current climate in senior living, if moving into a retirement home or long-term care home is in the plan, it is more important than ever before to be well prepared—even overprepared.

Here is what I mean by that. As you remember, there are very few suites/beds available if your loved one is planning on moving when and only when extensive care needs present themselves.

In long-term care, your loved one will usually be waiting for years when they finally get on the waiting list. By its own definition, long-term care expects you to wait until you require care that cannot be met in the community to qualify. However, seniors then need to wait sometimes years past that in order to actually receive access. So what does one do in the meantime? Most need to bring in family caregivers and home care, or make a move to a retirement home in the meantime.

But what if the retirement home system is also backed up with waiting lists, as it currently is? The best ways to get around that issue are as follows:

- Be open to choosing a retirement home that is not in the preferred location.
- Be prepared to go over budget, whether that is in the home itself or by bringing in additional care.
- Choose a home that does more care outside of the physical and memory care floors to broaden choices.
- Consider making a move earlier, when not as much care is required, so that your loved one can age in place and move internally.

BREADCRUMBS

You should also have a bit of a strategy around the time of year/season for the move. Often, retirement living follows the same spring and fall high seasons as real estate. If possible, look at securing a suite early, a few months before the rush. This may look like searching in February and July for move dates in April and September. Keep in mind that a lot of people look to move after "one last summer" or after a hard winter. To get the best choice of suite layouts, you need to be proactive and beat the crowds.

Individuals move for a variety of reasons, separate from care, including wanting more social interaction or needing help with nutrition and home upkeep. If these items are starting to pile up and you or the senior are becoming overwhelmed by it all, which often leads to exhaustion and stress and then may lead to isolation, please start looking into the process of a move if it's within the budget. As the caregiver in this situation, try to keep your personal feelings out of this and recognize that there isn't a cookie-cutter solution. If your loved one is struggling, start helping them move toward a positive solution. I touch on some objections around this in the next chapter.

KEY TAKEAWAYS

1. If your loved one is in a situation like the ones described in this chapter, it is very important to preplan.

2. Remaining at home can be great, but always keep an eye on the amount of renovation and care required and reevaluate as things change.

CHAPTER 10:

OPENING THE LINES OF COMMUNICATION

Opening the lines of communication in a family is crucial for fostering understanding, trust, and cohesion among its members. Effective communication allows family members to express their thoughts, feelings, and concerns openly, leading to healthier relationships and stronger bonds. When individuals feel heard and valued within the family unit, conflicts can be resolved more peacefully, and misunderstandings can be clarified. By prioritizing open communication, families can create a safe and nurturing environment where each member feels respected, validated, and connected.

Objections often arise when considering additional assistance or transitioning to a retirement or long-term care home. It may come as a surprise that some of these objections originate from seniors' children rather than the seniors themselves.

In this chapter, I will explore common objections seniors and adult children have and provide insights and guidance on assisting your loved one in overcoming their objections and fostering open lines of communication.

SITUATION: INDEPENDENT AND SICK OF IT!

Objector: Adult children or influencers

There are many individuals who are planners and look forward to a new and exciting chapter in their lives. For some, planning out their senior-housing journey is the natural next step. I have spoken to many who are ready and want to make a move to a retirement home but come up against unexpected objections from their adult children. These seniors are often independent and healthy enough to enjoy everything a retirement home has to offer, but they are sick and tired of household chores, meal planning and preparation, and social isolation. By embracing retirement living, these individuals really will get the best of both worlds by trading in their vacuums and spatulas for housekeeping services and dining with new friends.

Individuals in this group make a decision to move to retirement living well in advance, sometimes years before actually moving, and then proceed to take their time, do their homework, organize their affairs, and start to downsize.

OPENING THE LINES OF COMMUNICATION

Taking this approach allows individuals to grow into the idea of retirement living so that they are comfortable taking the next step of moving. Doing it this way often keeps stress to a minimum and allows individuals the time they need to sort through things, both in their home and their minds.

JOHN

John and I met one year before he decided to move. He was referred to me by a colleague who was assisting him with downsizing his house. When I spoke to John, he shared with me that his wife had passed away many years before and that his house was becoming too much for him. He was taking his time because he felt he had so many things to go through that he didn't want to be rushed.

The objection in this situation came from John's son, Adam, who often shared his opinions: "Dad, you're too young to move to a home," or "You're doing just fine in the house," or "But it's our family home."

Many seniors who make this decision experience hesitation, guilt, and outright negativity from their children. Family members of independent seniors are often not in agreement or are caught off guard when a loved one decides to downsize and move. This can be caused by the shock of the news and the thoughts of the inevitable in the future and by the child not being ready for this step in their own life.

The hurdle to get over in this type of situation is to figure out why the adult child has these opinions and where they stem from. These are some answers I've heard:

- "This was the home that I grew up in." In this case, the adult child is having a hard time separating from the physical home and the memories it's held.
- "My mom is not sick enough to be in one of those homes." This is often either caused by a lack of information about retirement living or the adult child's fears or unwillingness to face the fact that their loved one is getting older.

However, it is not only adult children who vocalize their feelings about a senior in their life making a move to a retirement home. Friends, other family members, and professionals often have an opinion as well.

SALLY

Sally was a healthy and independent woman. Recently widowed, Sally didn't drive and was becoming isolated. She was considering making a move to a retirement home and was starting to prepare herself for it. She had an issue, though: not knowing whether to move back to Montreal or stay in Ottawa was a huge problem for her. Worse yet, she shared with me that her doctor told her, "Don't you dare move into one of those homes!" This one ignorant comment made Sally have second thoughts and caused her even more stress surrounding her decision. As a result, she changed her mind about moving and continued to live in isolation.

In Sally's situation, she put a lot of trust in her family doctor, who clearly didn't understand seniors' housing. Unfortunately, Sally isn't alone, and I have seen this exact situation many times. It's especially sad when people do not have all the information and don't realize that their remark could have a lasting impression on an individual. This is specifically true for professionals, as many people put more weight into their opinions, especially if they have had a long-standing relationship.

SITUATION: ONE SENIOR REQUIRES CARE

Objector: Spouse or person requiring care

When one person starts to become ill, it's very common to see the caregiver pick up the slack when it comes to doing chores and providing assistance for their loved one. Their rationale? They do this out of love for their senior, because they want to stay in their family home for as long as possible—for themselves and, sometimes, for the kids—and because they usually don't expect the care needs to increase past what they can handle.

However, oftentimes in this scenario, the caregiver becomes completely burned out, emotionally spent, and physically exhausted. By the time we meet with them, they are almost at their wits' end.

One of two situations usually arises.

Option One

Situation: The *person* needing care requires a safer environment that can provide more care.

Objection: The *caregiver* does not want to move to a retirement home because they feel that they will be giving up their independence and think that they are fine and can continue on, or the thought of all the "stuff" is too much for them.

Usually, I find that the *caregiver* in this scenario is either the senior who is unsure of the unknown or someone who has worked in a caring profession (for example, a retired doctor or nurse).

In my experience, these individuals, while meaning well, cannot appropriately gauge how burned out they really are and refuse to "give up." Most often they have not considered the upside of moving. Often when in this situation, if a move were made, the caregiver would be freed up to have *more* independence as well as assistance with care for their loved one.

Option Two

Situation: The *caregiver* is completely burned out and wants to make a move.

Objection: The *person* requiring care does not want to move because they think everything is fine.

In this situation, the person *receiving* care often has some sort of cognitive decline and is being unreasonable because they don't understand and cannot see the magnitude of the situation. They can't see how much care they require, how exhausted their caregiver is, and how deeply their family is concerned for the welfare of both people.

I have also seen this happen when the person receiving care, who had no issues with their cognition, refused to move. Most often this was due to ego or the history of their partnership. In this type of situation, the caregiver is ready to make a move so they can live a less hectic and stressful life. I have also seen partners separate and the caregiver move to a home individually. What usually happens is the person requiring care cannot remain at home on their own and learns the hard way. The partners often reunite in the retirement home.

SITUATION: AN INDIVIDUAL REQUIRES TOO MUCH CARE TO REMAIN AT HOME ALONE

Objector: The senior themself

Most of the families I work with are looking for assistance in reasoning with their loved one that they can no longer remain in the home without care. The senior in this case is either refusing to bring in home care, refusing to move to a retirement home, or both. Family members often look for help with this situation after they are completely spent and can no longer help with the care. Unfortunately, this puts both the family members and their loved ones in danger. There are many ways to go about this situation. However, it really comes down to the individual family and whether or not the senior has a cognitive decline.

A possible solution could involve the family having an open and direct conversation with their loved one. Many do not want to do this, or feel as though they have already done so, but I would say, based on the thousands of families I have assisted over the years, that many beat around the bush and do not put up their own boundaries, or their conversations have turned into fights, over and over again. In situations where they have had a direct and thoughtful conversation, another solution is education. A lot of the time, the senior who does not want to move is scared or concerned about the move and needs more information on the steps that need to be taken, what retirement and long-term care really are, and what life might look like in a new home. I have even had people have the objection of not wanting to move because they thought *they* would have to be the person physically moving the belongings.

In the end, a direct and thoughtful conversation is the place to start. Make sure to empathize with your loved one. Share that you are scared or unsure as well, but that you will work through the next steps together.

OBJECTIONS AND HOW TO START UNPACKING THEM

Below are a few common objections I see with families. Let's discuss why they might come up and what you might say in a conversation to help unpack them with your loved one.

1. Retirement Homes Are Too Expensive

Fear of running out of money: Seniors might fear that the cost of retirement living and long-term care will deplete their savings and leave them without enough funds to support themselves in the future or to leave to their family after passing.

Unpack: "Would you be open to speaking with a financial professional as a first step to looking at the whole picture?"

2. You'll Never Get Me to Move into One of Those Old People's Homes

Misunderstanding the senior-housing and care industry: Lack of understanding about options and financial resources can lead to confusion and apprehension about how to afford necessary care.

Unpack: "Could we watch this short video/do some research on the topic so that we are both better prepared and educated? It would make me feel a lot less overwhelmed."

3. We Don't Talk About That / I Don't Want To Talk About That

Stigma surrounding mental health: Many individuals from older generations hold stigmatizing beliefs about mental health issues, making them hesitant to discuss their own emotional well-being.

Unpack: "I know that it can be uncomfortable to discuss sensitive topics, but I have noticed that you haven't been doing _____ anymore, and I'm worried."

4. Oh, It's Only One Fall

Denial or minimization: Some individuals may deny or downplay their physical health concerns, believing that they are just a natural part of aging or not worth addressing.

Unpack: "I agree—it's only one fall. Could we talk about what happened so that we can improve your living situation and fix any obstacles?"

5. I've Lived Here for 50 Years and Don't Want to Move from My Home

Emotional attachment: Some seniors have lived in their current homes for many years, creating a strong emotional attachment to their homes and their communities.

Unpack: "I know you have lived in this house a long time, and I am sad about this chapter coming to a close as well. However, we can preserve some of these memories while creating new ones."

6. I'm Perfectly Capable of Managing My Own Affairs and Don't Need Any Help

Avoiding emotional vulnerability: Some individuals might be uncomfortable discussing their emotions or fears, preferring to keep such matters private.

Unpack: "I know that you don't want to get into it, but I have a few concerns that I would like to share with you, and then we can leave it for a bit so you can think about it."

7. Retirement Homes Make You Play Bingo

Loss of independence: This senior values independence and fears that moving to a retirement home could mean losing control over their daily routine and decision-making.

Unpack: "I hear you! I wouldn't want to play bingo all day long either! I'm sure they do many other things—would you be open to looking at a sample activity calendar?"

8. Don't Bother Your Brother with This Paperwork—Let's Just Leave It Alone

Fear of family conflicts: This senior might be worried about family conflicts or disputes that could arise if they designate someone as their POA, fearing that this could cause division among family members. They would rather have no legal paperwork than work through the awkwardness.

Unpack: "Since we're your children, I know that Tim [brother] would be very upset if we did not share these details with him, as he also cares about you and wants the best for you. We will work together as a family."

OPENING THE LINES OF COMMUNICATION

THE ROLE STUBBORNNESS PLAYS

Stubbornness can and does play a huge role and contributes to all sorts of objections. I'm guessing this will resonate with many of you!

Some individuals would rather do things the way they always have, regardless of the fact that things around them are changing. The truth is, though, that it is impossible to keep things the same without these individuals being in danger or at serious risk. Again, this gets much worse when cognitive functions are declining.

RICHARD

I had a very brief meeting with Richard, a 52-year-old man living at home who was completely paralyzed. He had outside care coming in during the day but not at night. He was finding things very difficult with his physical limitations and total lack of social interaction. I was brought in to meet with him, as he had decided a few days prior that he should move, but upon my visit to his home, he had changed his mind again. All he wanted, he said, was to have a brief overview of the industry and to know the location of the retirement homes that could care for him. Unfortunately, all the homes that offered the very high level of care Richard so

> desperately needed were not in *his preferred location*, as he wanted to be in a place that would be convenient for his friend to visit. We spoke on and off for a month, and one day Richard's priest called to let me know Richard had fallen out of bed in the night and was not found for six hours. After many days in the hospital, Richard passed away in his home a few days later.

I wish I could say that Richard's case was rare or unusual, but unfortunately, it isn't. Despite wanting to act in someone's best interest, you can't make someone do something they don't want to do, especially when that person has not been deemed incompetent to make their own decisions. Richard used his friend's driving distance, as well as other objections, to provide a rationale for why he should stay in his home and not move anywhere else. But again, I say to this, "To what end?"

In other situations, such as where there is cognitive decline, the family has needed to activate a POA in order to move their parent because it was unsafe for the parent to remain living in their home.

The POA has a duty of care, and the person they are caring for has appointed them for just this reason, regardless of whether they remember why or agree with it later. Often, there is a lot of guilt on the part of the person who has the POA. In my experience, the person with the POA never truly wants to take on this role, but they are obligated to do so. When the rest of the family is not on the same page, that makes things even more complicated.

As a side note, many seniors I work with have not completed their POA documents or updated their wills. Please get this done! Other documents that are handy to have can be found in my estate planner (link at the end of the book). It makes everyone's life easier if they know the wishes of their loved ones.

FAMILY AND FRIENDS' OBJECTIONS

HENRY AND RUBY

One December 24th, I answered a call from a concerned daughter who wanted me to come and speak with her parents about making a move to a retirement home. She was getting more concerned about her mom specifically, and the day she called, she had just spent her fourth night in a row sleeping on the couch in her parents' living room.

We booked a meeting for the day after Christmas, with the daughter, her parents, and her brother. Throughout the conversation, we slowly got her father, Henry, on board with having a look at a few very specific retirement homes. Her mother, Ruby, was already interested in making a move—after all, she currently needed quite a lot of help.

After an hour-and-a-half-long conversation, Henry was at a point where he was willing to have an open mind and see a few homes. Promptly, his agreement was met by the son saying, "I just don't know about this. I know you aren't going to be happy living in a retirement home. You love your condo." Because of this, and drawing on his original objections, Henry backed down, and the family was immediately back to square one.

Sadly, four months later, it took failing health for both Henry and Ruby to make the move to a retirement home. They were sicker and more frail than they had been when I had originally met them at Christmas, when they had already been in a crisis situation.

I usually tell my clients to take others' opinions with a grain of salt. I also advise them to become informed.

More and more, seniors, like their children, are going online to get their information. Believe me when I say there is no lack of opinions when it comes to making decisions about retirement living! But there is also a lot of misinformation out there, and you need to ask the right questions.

OPENING THE LINES OF COMMUNICATION

Here's the thing: Most of the people who give their opinion (solicited or not) do not know, nor do they understand, the unique challenges you face. Many people feel that it's fine to toss out opinions and think there are no consequences in doing that, but there are—and those consequences can potentially be deadly.

The person who is asking for an opinion is usually stressed, confused, overwhelmed, and scared. They don't know where to start. This is a particularly delicate time where the senior or family member may be easily influenced by (what could be) a less-than-thoughtful opinion of someone who doesn't know or isn't thinking about the senior's entire situation. In my experience, the person looking for information will make an effort to go and see all the retirement homes suggested to them, with very little prescreening. When individuals are in this state and do not seek professional help, the average person will do this because they are afraid of making the wrong decision and think that more is better. Nothing could be further from the truth.

I often have people come up to me and say, "I chose the home for my mom after a lot of research and time…but I am still not sure I picked the correct one."

All this to say that, if you are a friend, be that. If you love them, support the person going through this huge change, and inform yourself of their ups and downs. It has nothing to do with you and everything to do with them.

If you are a family member, evaluate carefully and thoughtfully whether your loved one needs extra support with their decision-making. Don't make the assumption that they are not capable of making their own decisions, but be aware of what could be considered impaired judgment. Learn more about the situation, and try to truly understand the reasoning behind your loved one's thought process. They are still adults and have the ability—and the right—to make their own decisions. Be informed, be compassionate, and be thoughtful.

The exception to this is if they have given you or someone else the POA, and it's active. In this case, please see the section earlier in this chapter on POA.

FAMILY CONFLICT–CAUSED OBJECTIONS

I would say that in about 80% of interactions with families we assist, there is some sort of conflict, either between parent and adult child or between siblings.

Parent and Adult Child Conflict

These types of conflicts usually take one of two paths: the senior *doesn't* want to move, and their child wants them to;

or the senior *does* want to move, and the adult child does not want them to.

I touched on the latter previously, but just briefly. This conflict often arises when the independent senior chooses to make a move before their family is emotionally ready.

Whether it relates to selling the childhood home, money issues, or just the adult child's opinion, this type of conflict often leaves the senior feeling guilty or unsure, second-guessing themselves, or not knowing when or even if they should move. This can be especially stressful for seniors who have already invested time and emotion in making their decision. In addition, delaying the move can put the senior in danger in many different ways, including isolation, poor nutrition, and increased risk of falls.

In situations where a senior doesn't want to move and is still cognitively aware, but *you* think it may be better if they did consider moving, you might find campaigning for the move to be an uphill battle. As mentioned earlier, all of us are attached to our own way of life, and change is difficult. In this stage of life, many feel that when they move, it will be their "last move," which causes procrastination to be at an all-time high. It is very difficult to take a step forward when you are having to consider the end of your life.

BREADCRUMBS

As I mentioned earlier, one strategy I suggest to families is to never catch their loved one off guard. No one wants to be having Sunday dinner and get rocked with the statement "Mom, I think you need to move to a retirement home." *Whoa!* Unless you have a super hip mom, she will most likely run away screaming and put you up for adoption!

Book a time to have this conversation, maybe over tea. Inform your loved one of what you would like to discuss. This way, they can prepare themselves and put their thoughts, questions, and even rebuttals together. Those are all healthy responses, and your job is to do your homework and be prepared. Pushing will not help.

KAREN AND ELLIE

Karen contacted me after her dad passed away, as her mom, Ellie, was living in a large home, alone now, with a lot of stairs and clutter. Karen's dad used to help Ellie with the many pills she was on, and he would also help around the house. With her husband gone, Ellie was clearly struggling. Karen was having difficulty balancing her mom's needs with her own family as well as her work, and she was feeling very guilty over it. To top things off, Karen and Ellie had a strained relationship, which made having any conversations tricky.

OPENING THE LINES OF COMMUNICATION

> After Karen cleared it with Ellie, I was invited to Ellie's house to have a discussion, even though Ellie wasn't on board with making a move yet. Much of what I educated Ellie on was the general senior-housing industry, where I saw issues in her home, and what might be ahead of her in her health-care journey. After some time, Ellie was willing to have a look at some retirement homes.
>
> Spoiler—once I showed Ellie the first retirement home, she was sold. She put down a deposit and moved in a few weeks later. Her objections all wrapped around not understanding what was out there for retirement homes. She had thought that they were long-term care homes and was afraid to stray from what she knew, even though it wasn't working for her anymore.

Having "the talk" with a loved one can be challenging and scary. However, if you can get past that initial reaction of fear, you may uncover that the issue at hand is actually easier to address than you once thought.

Sibling Conflict

As for sibling conflicts…I have a sister—I get it! You will never agree 100% of the time, and when you have something as big as your parents' care on the plate, then you will most likely not agree completely.

When one sibling thinks their parents should move, another thinks they should not, and another is on the fence, the worst thing you can do is bring up this conflict in front of your parents. If the siblings are not united, the parent will usually do nothing. This is usually due to the senior not strongly wanting to move in the first place and having one or more of their children agreeing with them, casting doubt on the opinion of the adult child who thinks they should move.

Adult children often get frustrated because they know their loved one is in danger. They try to talk things over, but every conversation is met with "Look! I just did _____ (fill in the blank). I don't need to move anywhere! I'm fine on my own!" Having that same conversation over and over again is exhausting and time consuming. It keeps the senior in denial and, sadly, does nothing to move things in the right direction.

SUZANNE

Suzanne was a physically independent senior who used a walker and liked to leave it at the top of the stairs when she wanted to sit out on the patio. She would hold on to railings for dear life and furniture-walk, navigating her way down the stairs

OPENING THE LINES OF COMMUNICATION

and through her living room just to sit outside. Her family had moved most of her living room things to a sunroom on the main floor to try to limit her use of the stairs, but alas, Suzanne was a smoker, and the habit of sitting on the patio for a cigarette was ingrained in her bones.

When I was called in to meet with Suzanne and her two adult children, I found myself in the middle of a tug-of-war. The two children sat at the ends of the table, and Suzanne and I were sitting in the middle. Every time I tried to speak with Suzanne, the children ended up intervening, and an argument ensued.

The trouble with situations like this is that by the time I get called in to help, there have been *many* fights and disagreements, and a lot of tension has built up. Often, the adult children (or loved ones) are so scared, concerned, tired, overwhelmed, and desperate for a resolution that they are at a point of *demanding* instead of *asking*.

In my experience, seniors (parents) don't usually bend to that kind of pressure. It is better to have a strategy in place than to go in guns a'blazing. Now, I know many of you will think, *Well, I didn't plan to go in guns a'blazing at first, but that's where we ended up!* If there isn't a clear strategy developed beforehand, the situation can quickly go sideways.

The main type of sibling conflict I see is when an adult child is the main caregiver and there's another adult child who lives in another city, sometimes another province, state, or worse yet, out of the country, and the other child believes that they have a better pulse on what's happening with their parent(s). I'm saying "worse yet" to folks who are out of the country because health systems are completely different from country to country, and when people don't realize this or think they know better, it creates even more stress for the caregivers on the ground with the parents. Often, the opinion I hear from adult children who are not the main caregivers is that Mom and Dad are doing just fine and they don't need to move. Or I hear the complete opposite: that Mom and Dad need long-term care, when in fact their parents are not candidates for admission and sometimes they have not even applied to be assessed yet.

I've had siblings argue in front of their loved ones throughout our conversation. Others completely shut down and say nothing, giving their parents no support or direction. And still others stick their heads in the sand and deny that anything is wrong.

What's important is that you come to a compromise and present a united front. It's time to look at your own objections and reasons for them and educate yourself on the situation in order to assist your loved one in what can be a very tough decision.

KEY TAKEAWAYS

1. Objections can come from any member of the family/public, and it's important to weigh options and rely on what you feel your own needs are.

2. Education on senior living *always* helps. Don't be afraid to ask and research.

CHAPTER 11:

SENIORS WITH DEMENTIA

Strategies for Success

What a cruel disease this is. It can do any number of things to the human mind and body, and the uncertainty makes it difficult to plan for. Dementia can be particularly tricky as families attempt to move their loved one to a retirement or long-term care home.

I have come across many different situations where the individual with dementia is at a point where they need to make a move but haven't yet. Adult children tend to take on the parenting role, and regrettably, it usually doesn't go as planned.

While every situation is different, there are definitely some common variables.

BREADCRUMBS

PHYSICALLY INDEPENDENT SENIORS WITH DEMENTIA

I have worked with many families who have quite the challenge on their hands: their loved one is completely physically independent and healthy, but their mind is not.

CATHY

Cathy's family contacted me because Cathy, their physically fit, younger senior mom, was living on her own in a three-bedroom house on a busy street. The three kids visited Cathy as often as they could, supplying their mom with meals and helping with medications and general housekeeping. However, it was becoming more and more obvious that Cathy was in danger, and the siblings couldn't spend any more time helping as they all had young families of their own and full-time careers. The main concern: "Mom gets lost when she goes for a walk to the store, even though she is insistent that she knows where it is and how to get there. She doesn't understand that she shouldn't be leaving the house alone."

I arranged a meeting in Cathy's home with her and all three of her children to discuss the situation and the available options. Cathy did not want outside care services to come into her home because (in her words), she "didn't have enough for them to do." After all, in her own mind, she was very physically fit and could do all of her ADLs, housework, and meal prep on her own.

However, there was more going on. Her children were bringing in meals and, unbeknownst to Cathy, had unplugged the stove, as she had left the burner on a few times.

The solution in this situation was to make a move, and the family was investigating retirement homes.

Not being able to grasp the severity of the situation, Cathy did not understand why she needed to move and was not interested in speaking with me. After a little small talk, we were finally able to open the floodgates to all of her fears: leaving the family home she and her husband had shared with their children and not knowing anyone in a new place. Once we discussed all of this, we were finally at a spot where Cathy would consider touring—but only under the condition that I "promised not to leave her there" (after the tour). Once I could reassure her that of course I would not do that, she conceded.

We booked our tour, and wouldn't you know it, she loved the home and moved in a few weeks later.

> All of her fears seem to have vanished after she saw the home.

The biggest issue I see with seniors who have some form of dementia but are physically fit and live on their own is what the industry calls wandering. Their bodies are physically fit enough to walk everywhere, but their minds aren't fit enough to get them back home.

What about alert bracelets or pendants? Regrettably, in a wandering situation, having an alert bracelet isn't a successful option because the senior may forget to press the button, and many pendants don't have GPS. That being said, there are many other different types of locator devices on the market that use leading-edge GPS technologies. I urge you to investigate all options.

Often, when a senior moves into a retirement home with this type of situation, they need to live on the secured floor. It is the safest option for both the senior and the home.

MOBILITY-IMPAIRED SENIORS WITH DEMENTIA

In contrast to independently mobile individuals, there are different things to consider when the person requiring cognitive support also requires mobility support.

SENIORS WITH DEMENTIA

PETER

I met Peter, his wife, and his two children when they were trying to weigh out whether or not to move and when. Peter had a diagnosis of Parkinson's and had Lewy body dementia. His family was trying to weigh out how much of a continuum of care Peter would require in the future. The main issues were that Peter and his wife didn't want to move and that, if they did move, they were looking at independent apartments, separate from a retirement home.

I spoke at length about the progression of these two diseases and the fact that, if they moved to an apartment, I saw another move into a retirement home on a care floor in their near future. For Peter, we wanted to look for a full continuum of care in order to limit his number of moves. The home should have the ability to offer a two-person assist, and usually we would also look for a memory-care floor.

Peter's family had a choice to make. Since Peter's mobility wouldn't really allow him to become a wandering risk, they didn't necessarily need to choose a home with a secured floor. However, the cognitive programming on a floor like that could prove useful.

With physically debilitating dementia such as Lewy body, the individual loses a lot of mobility and usually doesn't require a secured floor. As with anything, there are always pros and cons to weigh out, and knowing the type of dementia will help you plan for future needs.

COMMUNICATING WITH LOVED ONES WHO MAY NOT REMEMBER CONVERSATIONS

When loved ones have memory issues, important conversations about care and living arrangements are even more difficult. How do you get them on the same page about a move?

Here are a few strategies. Pick up where you and your family are now, or try going back and starting again.

Upon noticing memory loss or in the early stages of the disease, ask your loved ones these questions, and have them write down their answers in their own handwriting (when possible):

When we feel that it is unsafe for you to remain in your home on your own, what are your wishes?

a. Do you want to move in with us?
b. Do you want us to bring in outside care?
c. Do you want to move to a retirement home/long-term care home?

d. If you move to a home, what would you like in a residence? (For example, a pool, a large suite, or a garden?)

Many parents don't want to be a burden to their children. However, as dementia creeps into more-advanced stages, it's important to understand that your loved one will not be reasoning in the same way as they may have before. The outcome to them could appear as "I'm getting kicked out of my house."

I have seen seniors who, before dementia, would never expect their kids to care for them. Then, after dementia progresses, they turn into demanding individuals who refuse every suggestion. One of the reasons they do this is because they are scared.

Consider that they most likely have "clear times" when they are aware that they are losing their memory—and think how terrifying that must be. Now pile on losing their home and many of their possessions. It's not hard to figure out why there is so much resistance. There are a few different ways to obtain assistance for your loved one who has dementia:

1. *Bring in outside care.* Bringing in care to help in the home can be tricky. When considering who to hire, it is important to be completely honest about your loved one's background, beliefs, and idiosyncrasies.

These won't change—if anything, their beliefs will be shined up and put up on display, unfiltered. For example, many of the seniors I work with have outdated points of views on race and gender roles and are very particular about who or what they like and don't like. It's often horrifying to adult children that their parents think and act like this. However, it's important to consider that this generation grew up in a different world than we live in now, and while their short-term memory may not be as intact, their long-term memory often is.

Don't worry. Home care companies, retirement homes, and long-term care homes are well aware of this and can work with you if you let them know about your loved one's idiosyncrasies up front. This will give everyone the best shot at setting up a respectful and successful relationship.

2. *A move to a retirement home or long-term care home.* I always find it best to do a preliminary search and bring options to the senior—but not a ton of options. One of the biggest problems with any senior who is in a situation that has many moving parts is that they are not sure where to begin or what needs to be done. So instead of having a *big* conversation about downsizing, moving, dealing with "their stuff," and so on, have a few smaller conversations

that are solution focused. Break it into smaller chunks. And keep in mind my earlier advice about siblings getting on the same page.
3. *Downsize.* Do your homework and present a solution instead of problems. Many seniors get stuck worrying about all the stuff they need to deal with. This, coupled with dementia, presents a huge mountain to climb. Also, many seniors feel that they are the ones who need to search through, pack, and get rid of everything single-handedly. They don't. And you don't either! There are some excellent downsizing companies out there with compassionate people who can help. Check them out and compare the options.

SHELLY

Shelly and I sat down late one January to discuss her plans for where and when to move now that her sister and roommate had passed away. She was lonely, and it was hard for her to get out and about in the winter.

When I asked Shelly about the timing of her move, she said, "Well, I think spring."

I replied, "After hearing that winter has been hard on you, why spring and not sooner?"

BREADCRUMBS

Her reply: "I don't want to move in the winter with all the snow and cold."

The next few words out of my mouth set everything in motion for her. "You know, it's not the same as when you were younger. Movers will come and do all the heavy lifting and organizing while I take you out for lunch. You can then arrive at your new home, all set up and waiting for you."

This information allowed Shelly the peace of mind to move within the next month.

4. *Move*. Again, do your homework. I'm a big fan of using an advisor—*wink, wink*—however, there is a strategy to moving. Be sure to consider where your loved one is now, both mentally and physically, and where they may end up as they age and as dementia progresses. It is important to know whether remaining in the same home as health deteriorates is the priority, or if making another move (to a different retirement home or a long-term care home) will work when care needs change. My suggestion is to tour some homes and identify the top two choices to discuss with your loved one. When you are at the point of touring, schedule a lunch and make an outing of it, doing only one tour a day. **Pro tip:** At every home you

tour, pay close attention to how your loved one reacts. This should give you a good idea of what they like. They may not remember later when you want to go over the options, so do as much discussing with them in the moment as possible.

Remember that moving can be challenging for any individual, but I have especially seen the difficulty when moving an individual with dementia. I find that it is best to limit the moves (do your research) and move sooner rather than later (so your loved one can have a better shot of getting adjusted).

On the other side of the coin are those families who have a loved one with dementia but may not have planned adequately. This might be for a variety of reasons. Perhaps the disease has moved quicker than expected. Maybe there is a lot of denial and stubbornness from the loved one. Or it could be that the family might not all live in the same city.

No matter what the circumstances, when there is an individual living on their own with progressing dementia, it is important to stay on top of what is happening in their life.

G-MA

I once dated a man whose grandma was facing some cognitive issues. When we went to visit

> her (she lived in another province), I noticed that she was forgetful—specifically, she was leaving the stove on, often. When I consulted with family members, they chose to remain in the dark and do nothing. This unfortunately didn't change for a number of years, and the advancing cognitive impairment resulted in a number of falls for G-ma. Today she is no longer physically independent and is being bounced between loved ones' homes, as no one wants to acknowledge the dementia and make decisions in her best interest.

Sadly, even when family members live in the same town, often they are in so much denial over what is happening to their loved one that they let the situation spin out of control. Many times, these families land in a position where they are enforcing an off-the-cuff plan instead of reinforcing an already-existing strategy.

If you find yourself in this situation, there are a few steps you can take to get your loved one into a safer, healthier setting.

1. *Speak with them.* Depending on how much clarity your loved one may still have, having a conversation with them about what is happening and what your concerns are can go a long way. It is important not to blame your loved one or make them feel guilty (if, say, you have been taking care

of them). Avoiding tough conversations only reduces clarity and increases behaviors that are undesirable. Said another way: if you don't face the problems in a direct manner, then the person with dementia won't know exactly how you feel, and that leaves room for negotiation. This approach also includes getting on the same page as the rest of the family and bringing a united decision/discussion to your loved one.

When people with dementia are in a situation where they don't have a say in their pending upheaval, this can result in difficulties for everyone. If you don't spend time addressing fears and feelings, or if you don't have conversations that lead to a safe change, then you will spend an excessive amount of time feeling guilty, stressed, and upset. Your loved one may also experience anger, outrage, sadness, frustration, and a host of other emotions. So be brave. Be proactive. Have those conversations.

2. *Bring in professionals.* Whether it be for mediation, moving, or anything in between, in my experience, if you can put a professional in between you and your loved one, then the outcome will be better. Even though your loved one has dementia, they will still want to be heard and acknowledged. Often

the adult children try to repeatedly force a decision instead of coming to a decision together (even if the loved one won't remember it very well). When I get called in to mediate and advise, my focus is 95% on the senior and 5% on the adult children. I use that 5% to confirm the validity of what is being said so that I can move the conversation forward in a positive way for the senior.

3. *Invoke a POA.* Sometimes, the only thing you can do is have an active POA and enforce it. Bottom line—if your loved one is in danger and incapable of making safe decisions, you need to make the decision for them. I understand that this is not an ideal or easy situation, and the few clients of mine who have had to do this have felt tremendous stress, guilt, and sadness. However, if you try to separate yourself from being the daughter/son/family member, take on the POA role responsibly, and do what your judgment tells you is best for your loved one, then you should not feel guilty. Let yourself feel relieved. Rest a bit. Let's face it: By the time you get to the stage of using the POA, you are probably burned out and exhausted from caring and worrying. Take heart in knowing you are doing the best thing you know how to for your loved one.

SENIORS WITH DEMENTIA

MELANIE AND EDNA

> Melanie called me up one day late last year as her mom, Edna, had fallen and had been on the floor for four hours before being found and taken to the hospital. Edna was lucky enough not to have major injuries, but the doctors didn't think that she should return home due to her increasing dementia and poor decision-making. Of course, Edna thought she was fine and resisted moving. However, Melanie took this opportunity to call me to see what I could do.

In a situation like this, it is often not a good idea to have your parent move back home after they have been in the hospital. I have found, more often than not, that the amount of fighting escalates, and it is almost always harder to get Mom to move out of the house. Many families choose to move their loved one right from the hospital in order to reduce the resistance. On some occasions, we have framed it for the loved one as going to a retirement home for a respite for rehab or convalescence before they could return home. In Edna's case, that's what her family did. After a few weeks, we found that Edna had calmed down and become immersed in the retirement home community.

BREADCRUMBS

DECISION-MAKING AND REASONING

JENNY

One morning I went to visit Jenny and her daughter, Carla, after speaking with Carla and her brother over the phone about their concerns for their mom.

Jenny, 101, was living in her home of 30 years and was starting to have increasing mobility and personal-hygiene issues. She had a caregiver with her from 8 AM to 11 PM every day and was alone overnight. She also had multiple flights of stairs that I watched both her and the care worker struggle to come down the day I visited. While I was with Jenny and Carla, the red flags that I saw and discussed included the carpet being a risk when using the walker, the likelihood of a fall if Jenny got up in the middle of the night to use the bathroom, and the fact that, when they went out, Carla was the person supporting Jenny by holding her arms, which meant that the likelihood of one slipping and taking the other one out was high. Additionally, Jenny had already had four falls, resulting in her breaking various body parts, and her husband had had a fall in the same home and had gone to a retirement home because of it, but that didn't even faze Jenny.

In my experience, red flags like these would usually cause someone to be more active after our talk. But given that Jenny was not moved by these things, and considering the repetitive nature of our conversation and the fact that she was willing to stay in the home until something happened, that told me that if the POA was active, Carla should be looking at making a decision on Jenny's behalf, as I didn't think she had enough capacity left to make a proper decision and weigh out all the facts.

Unfortunately, this type of situation is not new to me. There are many family members out there who don't want to be the decision-makers, and instead they leave it to the person with the cognition impairment to make decisions. I can't stress this enough: If the POA is activated, there is a reason for it. Please don't let a situation like this drag on because you don't want to make the decision yourself or don't want to feel like the bad guy.

KEY TAKEAWAYS

1. Having a diagnosis of dementia requires an added layer of strategy.

2. Dementia progresses differently for everyone, so use the disease guidelines to help estimate future care.

FINAL WORDS

I know that taking in this much information might have felt like drinking water from a fire hose, but my hope is that as you digest it, you will feel a little less stressed and overwhelmed, as you now have a strong grasp on the world of Eldercare and senior housing. This book is designed to offer you strategies in many different situations so that you can start and continue important conversations with your loved ones. Remember: whether it's independent living, fully assisted living, memory care, or long-term care, every situation is unique and needs a unique approach.

You are not alone! Many families have similar struggles to those that you may be facing. Sometimes you just need to open up a conversation with a friend, neighbor, or colleague to see that you're both working through similar things. There are also always professionals available to assist you in pretty much all aspects of your search and decision-making, whether it be finance, real estate, downsizing, moving, or retirement living. Lean on these people, as they will be able, at the very least, to direct you on what your next steps might look like.

BREADCRUMBS

Should you need some additional support, I have included some resources for you at the back of this book.

If you are in the Ottawa area, Tea & Toast is always available to help you navigate the industry and offer referrals for additional services. Visit us at www.teaandtoast.ca.

If you are in Canada and need assistance, my group of Eldercare planners is available to help as well. Visit us at www.eldercareplanning.ca.

Take care of yourself and each other.

Warmest regards,

Amy

WHERE ARE THEY NOW?

"Anna and Mary" are still working with their parents to come to a decision about timing and location.

"Flo and Roger" decided that they weren't ready for a retirement home just yet. They decided to take an apartment and keep an eye on the situation.

"Maggie" decided to stay in her condo, after many respite stays in different retirement homes.

"Vic" moved to a retirement home to get the support he needed. After a few months, he was able to move into a long-term care home, where he resides now.

"Ruth and Robert" remained in their home with a promise to reach out to their children for more assistance.

"Mark" still has his mom living with him. They have brought in additional care and modified the home to be safer.

"Mavis" is currently in respite care with plans to move home with her son in a few weeks.

"Bert and Jane" chose to stay home for the time being and ease into a move by working on decluttering first.

BREADCRUMBS

"John" happily moved into a very independent residence where he would be well cared for now and able to move into the adjoining building when his care needs increase, giving him a full continuum of care.

"Sally" is still stuck between moving to Montreal or Ottawa but is planning a stay in Montreal in the very near future.

"Richard," sadly, passed away.

"Henry and Ruby" have signed their lease and are moving into a retirement home!

"Ellie" chose to move to the retirement home and lived there until she passed away. Ellie and Karen enjoyed a renewed relationship that was positive and fulfilling.

"Suzanne" ended up choosing a retirement home after her first tour. She lived there until her care increased, then we moved her to another retirement home to live out the rest of her life.

"Cathy" only needed one tour to be comfortable with a move. She started on a more independent floor, but after being monitored by the home, she was moved to a secured floor, where she continues to reside today. I have been told that Cathy's attitude has changed, as she is less stressed because she needs to make fewer decisions now.

WHERE ARE THEY NOW?

"Peter" is still trying to convince his wife to move and has decided that when the move comes up, they will look for a home with a continuum of care.

"Shelly" moved to the retirement home that very winter, and every time I see her, she is smiling and laughing with her new peer group!

"G-ma" still lives with her loved ones.

"Melanie and Edna"—Edna went into a retirement residence for a short stay, and in the end, she loved the home and made a lot of new friends. She is still at the same retirement home.

"Jenny" is still in her home and has had a few more hospital visits. Her daughter and son are currently making a plan for a crisis move and they have put in a stair lift as well as 24-hour Home care.

ABOUT THE AUTHOR

Amy Friesen is widely recognized as a luminary in the field of senior living, celebrated for her diverse roles as a best-selling author, educator, and expert. In 2014, driven by a profound dedication to enriching the lives of seniors and their families worldwide, Amy founded Tea & Toast, a pioneering initiative aimed at providing invaluable support in navigating the complexities of housing and health care for seniors.

Tea & Toast serves as a testament to Amy's unyielding commitment to fostering better choices and alleviating the often overwhelming burdens associated with Eldercare. Amy's holistic approach to client care not only prioritizes clients' immediate well-being but also facilitates seamless transitions throughout the Eldercare journey, infused with compassion, empathy, and seasoned expertise.

The unique methodology employed by Tea & Toast has become a beacon of hope for countless families, offering personalized assistance tailored to individual needs and aspirations. By meticulously planning for short and long-term goals, Amy and her team alleviate the stressors inherent in Eldercare, allowing families to navigate this pivotal phase with confidence and peace of mind.

In addition to her groundbreaking work with Tea & Toast, Amy is the visionary behind a cross-Canadian association of Eldercare Planning professionals, advocating for caregiver support, senior living, and comprehensive aging solutions.

Amy's leadership in the senior housing industry has earned her widespread recognition, including the prestigious 2018 Businesswoman of the Year, and *Ottawa Business Journal's* 2019 Forty Under 40 Award, both acknowledged by the House of Commons.

Amy's influence extends far beyond her professional accolades, permeating the various media platforms where she has been featured in numerous news interviews and sought after as a guest on podcasts. Through these channels, she generously shares her wealth of knowledge and insights on senior living and Eldercare Planning, enriching discourse and understanding.

APPENDIX

For those interested in delving deeper into the topics covered in the book, all the mentioned resources are conveniently available at www.amyfriesen.com/breadcrumbs-resources

The Tea & Toast website hosts an extensive array of supplementary materials including articles, multimedia content, and additional resources curated to provide further insights into the subjects discussed. Please visit www.teaandtoast.ca/resources

For individuals throughout Canada, Eldercare Planners of Canada is a great resource to find assistance in your area. Please visit www.eldercareplanning.ca

www.ingramcontent.com/pod-product-compliance
Lightning Source LLC
LaVergne TN
LVHW010821150225
803821LV00031B/1082